MW00618198

Charismatics In Crisis
Testing the Spirit of Prophets and Prophecy

ISBN: 978-1-7330564-8-9(Paper Back)

Book Design and Authorship by Don Pirozok
Editor Cheryl Pirozok

First Printing 2021 Amazon Publishing, United States

Published By: Pilgrims Progress Publishing
Spokane Valley WA. 99206
Website: www.donpirozok.com

Introduction

I have been part of the Charismatic Movement for a better part of thirty-seven years. I was baptized in the Holy Spirit with the Charismatic experience of speaking in unknown tongues in 1981. I have seen the good, the bad and the ugly in those years having ministered inside of the Movement for at least thirty-five of those years. One thing I can vouch for is Charismatic's are high on the experiential side of the Christian faith. Of course, many Charismatics have come out of what has been considered dry institutional Churches which teach the gifts of the Holy Spirit like the speaking of tongues has passed away. So, when Charismatics receive the Baptism of the Holy Spirit and speak in tongues many are ignited and propelled into serving the Lord. No real formal training into doctrines, or in-depth Bible study, often results in pushing experiences with young Charismatic's. The attempt to depart from dry formalism into a dynamic life in the Holy Spirit is often the motivation.

In this way Charismatics might say experiences outweighs those who only have Bible knowledge without experience. In some cases, this is true. For example, a man who sits inside of an institutionalized Church having never been born again, hearing good solid doctrine on Salvation, but never coming into saving faith. Another example would be Evangelical cessationists who argue tongues have passed away with the first century Church. Since Charismatics have the experience of speaking in tongues this argument appears silly. Their experience outweighs the Evangelical doctrine of cessationism.

However, herein lies the danger of Charismatic experiences, both the born-again experience and the baptism of the Holy Spirit is proven by Scriptures as the first century Church was definitely Charismatic by experience and taught both doctrines. After those two experiences extra, Biblical phenomena needs to be highly discerned as many counterfeits come from the demonic world. Evil spirits attempt to counterfeit the presence of God to influence Charismatics who are continually seeking experiences. This is where gross errors and have come into the 21st century Charismatic Movement. Without proper grounding in sound doctrines, the Charismatic Movement has fallen into strange manifestations, accepting them as the work of the Holy Spirit.

So dangerous has become this deception many who stand outside of the Charismatic Movement have now labeled the deception as strange fire. This labeling comes from the Bible in the Old Testament where the sons of Arron offed a perverse sacrifice to the Lord which was called by God strange fire. The story of this offering is recorded in Leviticus:

Leviticus 10:1-3

1 And Nadab and Abihu, the sons of
Aaron, took either of them his censer, and
put fire therein, and put incense thereon, and
offered strange fire before the Lord, which he
commanded them not.
2 And there went out fire from the Lord, and
devoured them, and they died before the Lord.
3 Then Moses said unto Aaron, This is it that
the Lord spake, saying, I will be sanctified in them that
come nigh me, and before all the people I will be
glorified. And Aaron held his peace.

For now, suffice us to say legitimate priests of God
offered an unholy sacrifice which perverted the way
God was to be worshipped. The cost of perverting God's
worship was the death sentence. Which demonstrates
even though men can be chosen and anointed by God
to help lead the Church, they can also fall into
perverting the way of the Lord. This unholy worship is
considered strange fire by the Lord, and defiles the
worshipers resulting in God's judgment against their
lives.
Now today inside of the Charismatic Movement many
who are considered chosen by God and anointed as
leaders within the Movement, are being confronted
about leading the Church into worshiping God with
strange fire. So dangerous is this practice entire
Evangelical communities have arisen to warn of the
Charismatic deception, and a great debate has ensued
between Charismatics and Evangelicals. However, many

Charismatics have refused to take the warnings and correction seriously as Evangelicals also tend to attack authentic experiences in Charismatics like speaking in tongues. This book is written from my experience coming from inside the Movement, where the Lord began to awaken me to the dangers of Charismatic strange fire.

Hope this testimony will help many Charismatics. To see the danger without throwing away the Charismatic experience. In order to write on this difficult issue, I have chosen not to name the leaders, or name of their different Charismatic Movements. Instead, only to expose their practice and deceptive teachings. In this way Charismatics will not have to rise up and defend their favorite apostle or prophet whose practice has become strange fire. Instead, they can consider the facts and judge for themselves if the warning should be heeded for their lives. I do however post examples from the Charismatic leaders who are in error.

Where I Started

Here I am a Charismatic tongue talking Christian, I have experienced the Baptism of the Holy Spirit. Before then I never knew God had power or experience for those who would follow Jesus Christ. Now I can see for myself by experience, God has given us the Holy Spirit, and the presence of God can be experienced. However, what I never knew was the amount of spiritual warfare which would also come with Holy Spirit baptism. After all I was introduced into a whole new world of living in the Spirit, so walking in the Spirit was a lesson to be learned.

My hunger for God was growing daily with this new experience of Holy Spirit power, and now I learned there were other gifts of the Holy Spirit like prophecy, and healing. So, I pushed into searching out those gifts, and was around other hungry Christians who sought them too. The gifts of the Holy Spirit required us to take risks, which in the beginning we were afraid to mistakes. In those days, the Holy Spirit was beginning to emphasize the gift of prophecy, so the Charismatic Church was on a large learning curve. In those days just a few men were proficient in the gift of prophecy to be considered accurate enough to be called New Testament prophets.

I was only a few years in the Lord, was with a youth movement which emphasized making new disciples, and personal discipleship. It was also called the Shepherding Movement by those outside, who saw the control and manipulation which came from the leaders inside the Movement. However, I was young in the Lord, and eager to serve the Lord in some kind of ministry. Many of us young college age students would share our faith on University campuses. Inside our particular brand of Shepherding was a growing acceptance of prophecy and developing the Holy Spirit gifts of revelation. Every time an accomplished prophet came to minister to our local body, my heart would really beat with resonance, as I felt I would also minster prophetically someday.

While that day came sooner than later, as the gift of prophecy seemed to grow and develop quickly in my life. I began to prophesy inside corporate meetings and then to individuals. I came to learn the level of accuracy was at a high level, and the people I spoke over prophetically confirmed the words I had spoken by revelation. Within several years I would be using the prophetic gift on a continual and constant basis. Which eventually led to an itinerate ministry, moving through the Charismatic Movement ministering in personal prophecy.

In those years, many things were spoken in the name of the Lord and would become normal practice inside the Charismatic Movement. Some observations could be made from personal experiences: 1) a man's ability to minster in the gifts of the Holy Spirit, is in no way indicative of his character. 2) a prophetic person can be highly gifted, and still struggle with sin, and corrupted practices. 3) In the past the prophetic Movement has tended to excuse the sin, and poor character of highly gifted prophetic people.

I want to confess, what was allowed in the prophetic Movement in the early days has set the foundation of corruption in the Movement today. The Charismatic Church went further and further into experiences, seeking words of prophecy, and pressing into seeking spiritual encounters. In this way the prophetic ministry became something which God never intended. It was exalted Into a place where meetings consisted of hours of personal prophecies. Now this practice begin to be very dangerous, because prophecy was being treated as if could happen upon demand. Instead, the Biblical gift of prophecy, it began to be the ability to read people, know their thoughts and desires, and speak into those desires as if you were receiving special revelation from the Lord.

Those were the early days when psychic ability began to grow inside the prophetic ministry. The boundaries which protected the Church from the excess and errors of the prophetic gifts was quickly dissolving, and powers of the soul, psychic ability was quickly growing. Now without restraints in place, the door opened to the supernatural in a greater way, and familiar spirits of occult, and New Age witchcraft brought prophetic experiences to a new level.

However, by this time New Testament prophets were highly revered and entire conferences which featured the prophets drew thousands of loyal Charismatics. It was at this time the Holy Spirit really began to warn of a greater deception coming from the prophetic ministry. It was like you could be in a meeting, called out by name, or given your birth date, and then receive a completely false prophecy. However, the details were so accurate, no one was considering the prophets were off, and evil spirits were invading the Movement. What also grew during this time was an alarming number of subjective revelations coming from the pulpit which were being preached as doctrine. In this way the Prophetic Movement began to grow in a large amount of false prophecy and false doctrine.

In the next ten years an explosion of corruption would come into the whole prophetic movement. Prophecy was so popular it began to be marketed as a product to be packaged and sold. Many prophets who were gifted in personal prophecy began to manipulate the Church using prophecy for personal financial gain. Also, prophetic conferences were being marketed where promises to train anyone who wanted to become proficient in speaking prophetic words. It was like the prophetic gifts were being wholesaled to the Church with promises of supernatural abilities for all.

Then came what was called the Extreme Prophetic. Which from the very beginning looked more New Age than the Biblical gift of prophecy. It promised visions upon demand, astral travel into heaven, communication with angels, and even communication with Old Testament people in heaven like Moses and Elijah. Schools of the supernatural were packaged and marketed, where all restraints were thrown off. Supernatural experiences were fostered by New Age techniques, like guided visual imagery. Today all over the world, the Extreme Prophetic is ministered as if is the authentic work of the Holy Spirit. However, evidence of gross corruption are being evidenced everywhere.

A whole language of values has arisen to support where the Extreme Prophetic has gone. The language represents the doctrinal belief prophetic people can access heaven upon demand. Belief in heavenly visions and visitations flood the prophetic culture within the Charismatic prophetic community. From Jacobs Ladder to heavenly portals, to the open heavens, Christians are taught to bring Heaven to Earth by prophetic experiences. Combined with a worldwide Christianizing of nations, the Prophetic Movement has become Joel's Army, a great end time super Church of miracle workers. All this belief and practice is become an everyday event in the Charismatic Church where the prophetic ministry has evolved over the last thirty years into a Christian New Age influenced Movement.

We have come to a place we must seriously examine the Charismatic Prophetic Movement In light of its growing New Age Influences. I will attempt to break down some of the internal practices and doctrinal beliefs in order to expose the strange fire of the New Age inside the Movement and promoted by its high visibility leaders. Now having come from inside I have seen firsthand many of these issues. I hope for the entire Movement to take seriously the confrontation which has going on for years from those outside the

Movement. Now Charismatics who have been involved on the inside, are also beginning to speak out like myself as God is exposing the deception before more Christians are moved into worshiping with the strange fire of the false prophetic.

Chapter One
The Prophetic Movement Is Called On the Carpet

Now that Charismatic prophets have finally decided Trump will not be reelected the song and dance begins as to the reasons why the prophets deceived millions with false predictions. You must remember the whole Prophetic Movement has been charged with error and deception now for almost two decades. Most of the names who are revered as prophets have given false predictions over the course of many years. However, these words were simply buried under the great volume of false prophecies the entire Movement has given for years. Let us be frank, an elitist superiority mentality has dominated the prophets whenever they were being confronted. They insist they knew better than everyone else, and often warned of not touching Gods anointed. Except they were in the flesh, attempting to say I had a vision, a dream, an angel, or Jesus came to me. Therefore, they though they held special privileges in the body of Christ which the average Joe in the Church did not have with God. In the end we see Satan tempting the prophets with good old fashioned "you are really a great prophet from God," and hold the secrets which can change the world.

Many who say they are prophets are not prophets at all. Some are simply good a speaking and moving crowds by their particular style of manipulation. Some are businessmen who have no right to dictate direction, and doctrine in the body of Christ. These false prophets has brought in psychology, philosophy, and business techniques into the Church to create and audience and following. Some of the false prophets adopted the philosophy of the 7 Mountains Mandate and have marketed this corruption during the whole of the Trump Presidency. A false Gospel largely responsible for developing the idolatry which lifted up the President into an unnatural position before America, and before God. Now that the house of 7 Mountain cards has come tumbling down, and the nation is divided by Charismatic Christians seduced into following this philosophy.

What is sadly missing from the prophets of the Apostolic/Prophetic Charismatic Movement is true discernment and accountability. When they are proven wrong, they simply run to their prophetic friends who have told them its ok, and just move forward. In this way the deem they are men and women under authority. However, their false prophecies and lying visions speak otherwise as they are not submitted to the Head of the Church Jesus Christ. Just because your buddy in ministry has a title of apostle or prophet does not mean their ministry is from God, or they are under Christ's authority.

Some are truly called as New Testament prophets. Why are they gone to such extremes in making such bold false predictions and using their gift to deceive the Church? First of all, they were being tempted to be someone great. They projected their need using worldly fame and success as their model to identify. However, true prophets must identify with Jesus Christ and the Cross. True prophets must suffer shame and reproach for the offense of the Cross. In the most developed of apostles and prophets is the measure of suffering for Christ and being considered a fool in the eyes of the world. Simply put many who would be called true prophets compromised the gifting for worldly fame, fortune, and glory. It will take a deeper death to self-laying down their gifting on the altar of God so it can be burned up by the Lord then resurrected into real prophetic character and ministry.

False prophets abound because most were not called by God to be New Testament Prophets. The same goes for apostles who are called by God and are popular motivational speakers. The Charismatic Prophetic Movement has wreaked havoc on the Church and American politics by false apostles and prophets who transformed themselves and were never called by God. As the Charismatic prophets begin to confess some level of error and deception in light of years of failed predictions, many will simply refuse to lay down their falsehood and continue to practice their illegitimate ministries. Their repentance from dead works will not be real, and at the Judgment Seat of Christ will lose the right of Kingdom age rewards. The Lord Jesus Christ pronounces judgment upon the false prophets who have prophesied, who worked miracles, and who cast out evil spirits, but were illegitimate ministries; "depart from Me you workers of iniquity for I never knew you."

Matthew 7:13-23

13 Enter ye in at the strait gate: for wide is the gate, and broad is the way, that leadeth to destruction, and many there be which go in there at:
14 Because strait is the gate, and narrow is the way, which leadeth unto life, and few there be that find it.
15 Beware of false prophets, which come to you in sheep's clothing, but in wardly they are ravening wolves.
16 Ye shall know them by their fruits. Do men gather grapes of thorns, or figs of thistles?
17 Even so every good tree bringeth forth good fruit; but a corrupt tree bringeth

forth evil fruit.

18 A good tree cannot bring
forth evil fruit, neither can a corrupt tree bring
forth good fruit.

19 Every tree that bringeth not forth good fruit is hewn
down, and cast into the fire.

20 Wherefore by their fruits ye shall know them.

21 Not everyone unto me, Lord, Lord, shall
enter into the kingdom of heaven; but he that doeth the
will of my Father which is in heaven.

22 Many will say to me in that day, Lord, Lord, have
we not prophesied in thy name? and in thy name have
cast out devils? and in thy name done many wonderful
works?

23 And then will I profess unto
them, I never knew you: depart from me, ye that
work iniquity.

What Makes Correcting Charismatic Movement So Difficult

It is well known inside the Charismatic Movement a
great deal of false practices, and false doctrines have
arisen. I have come from inside the Movement and have
seen many of the issues firsthand for years. So why such
a controversy, such a divide, inside and outside the
Movement?

1) I trust the majority of the people inside the Movement are sincere and are truly Christian. Attacking the salvation of people inside the Movement is not the right direction. Here is a fact, you can be born again, and still be deceived, and follow false teachers. To say, the people who lead the Movement have never been saved is to complicate the issue. Even the Christians who came out of the Movement, finally understanding the deception and error where themselves saved inside the Movement before the came out. The issue is not unbelievers acting like Christians, instead believers which are deceived by false doctrines and practices.

2) Correcting real born-again Charismatic Christians is difficult because they know they have Christ in their lives. They know they are forgiven and have New Life in Christ. A Christian, who is in deception is hard to correct because they are in the flesh, but believe they are following the Lord. Notice in the Scriptures heresy is listed as a work of the flesh:

Galatians 5:20
20 Idolatry, witchcraft, hatred, variance, emulations, wrath, strife, seditions, heresies,

3) The Charismatic Movement has fallen to heresy, false doctrines, and false practices is in the flesh, and not the Spirit. The problem has become a mutual agreement inside the Movement not to receive correction for works of the flesh. The real issue then is the low spiritual standards, which are set and allowed by leaders inside the Movement. For Christians who walk in integrity transparency, exposure, correction is common and normal practices for Christians who are walking in the Spirit. Anyone who is a Christian who reuses correction or does not want their flesh exposed will fall to deception and works of the flesh.

4) One leader inside the Movement will not confront and expose other leaders in sin and error. In the past even when high visible leaders were known to be in sin, other leaders protected them from exposure, and helped in the cover up. A practice of secrecy, and false correction where deep rooted sin, and works of the flesh are excused and overlooked. The main reason is pride, and idolatry of ministry. Some have been so exalted by the Movement, they are deemed just to "gifted and anointed," to hold to true Biblical morals and standards.

5) Without confrontation and correction, the flesh becomes proud and elitist, self-exalted, self-

glorying. Sadly, this portion of the Charismatic Movement views itself as more spiritually advanced than those outside the Movement. It is deceived by its own idolatry and pride. The Movement has made an idol out of its own image. No one is allowed to break the delusion, to bring exposure and correction. Deceived leaders are lifted up to think highly of themselves to be great apostles who will convert the whole know world. They have become legends unto themselves and tell one another how great their ministries are. The only standard of measurement they allow, is to compare themselves by themselves.

6) Those outside the Movement who are not Charismatic, who do not speak in tongues can compound the issue. First, they often say the leaders themselves are not saved. A belief one cannot be saved unless Charismatic leaders preach a true Gospel, makes the issue more complicated. The Second issued by non-Charismatics is to attack the real gifts of the Holy Spirit, like speaking in tongues. It is clear from Scriptures speaking in tongues was a common practice of the first century Church. So, speaking in tongues is considered a work of the Holy Spirit, and not demonic babble, or human ingenuity, or religious deception. Part of the problem among Evangelicals who do not speak

in tongues, is to attack the gifts of the Spirit which are Biblical, which Evangelicals teach stopped after the first century Church.

7) You are not in deception because you speak in tongues. Throwing out the baby with the bath water, is not correct either. So, Evangelicals often automatically think if a person speaks in tongues, they have been deceived. Even though Evangelicals are correct in identifying false doctrines, and false practices, they are wrong in the matter of tongues, and continuation of the gifts of the Holy Spirit.

8) A Christian can be born again, speak in tongues, and follow a false teacher, and false doctrines, and think they are following Jesus Christ being led of the Holy Spirit. That is what makes correction of deception in the Charismatic Movement a problem. As much of what is authentic in Christ is used to excuse and cover up the excess and errors.

9) Of course, Satan and evil spirits are involved pulling the wool over Charismatic Christians eyes.

You Have A Religious Spirit

What happens when you confront Charismatic Christians who are following the false doctrines of their favorite Charismatic apostle? Comparing the written Word of God, and the proper doctrines of Jesus Christ, against false doctrines and subjective revelations. Often the response is not with Bible doctrine to clarify their true Bible position. Instead, many often say to the Christian who is doing the confronting, "you have religious spirit, or you are a religious Pharisee." In essence their countering is not about the Scriptures, instead "you are wrong," or not credible. Their statement is not in defense of proper doctrine, often Charismatics who are confronted give no accounting to their false doctrines. The Written Word is not their argument of defense on the basis of Scripture, instead an accusation of religious spirit has influenced your confrontation of our lives.

Is it proper for Charismatic Christians to use the "you have a religious spirit tactic," to those who are being confronted with false doctrines and practices? Here is the reality? Any Christians who stands on the Word of God asking for an accountability to false doctrines does not have a religious spirit. Instead, they are standing on the high ground of "the truth," as compared to lies and deception. When being confronted with the truth a common tactic is to use "Ad Hominem." Instead of answering to the charges of deception based upon the ultimate authority God's Word. Many Charismatics who refuse the exposure of their false doctrines often turn to attack the person confronting, by attacking their character.

It is a form of misdirection, taking the focus off the real issue of deception, attempting to discredit the person as unreliable, a defective person with a suspect character.

(Quote from Wikipedia)
Ad hominem (Latin for "to the person"[1]), short for argumentum ad hominem, is a fallacious argumentative strategy whereby genuine discussion of the topic at hand is avoided by instead attacking the character, motive, or other attribute of the person making the argument, or persons associated with the argument, rather than attacking the substance of the argument itself.[2] The terms ad mulierem[3] and ad feminam[4] have been used specifically when the person receiving the criticism is female.

Now let us look at the real religious spirit. The Pharisaical person is a religious leader in the days of Jesus Christ who "made the Word of God of no effect, by their religious behaviors and traditions. Did you get that a religious spirit, or a Pharisee does not keep the Word of God, instead by religious systems, and manmade traditions, philosophies invalidate God's written Word and Commands? So, the argument given by Charismatics when being confronted by twisting Gods written Word by false doctrines and popular new light teachings is in reality a confrontation of the religious spirit.

In this case attacking the confronting person with the charge, you have a religious spirit, without admitting you are not holding to the true doctrines of Christ is in essence the very religious denials of old time Pharisees. The person who is accusing the Christian standing on the Word of God, is actually the person deceived by false religious beliefs. In this case their statement is 100% completely the opposite of what they accuse. They are being the religious Pharisee using religious pride to cover up their errors and deception.
.

Matthew 16:1-12

The Pharisees also with the Sadducees came, and tempting desired him that he would shew them a sign from heaven.
² He answered and said unto them, When it is evening, ye say, It will be fair weather: for the sky is red.
³ And in the morning, It will be foul weather today: for the sky is red and lowering. O ye hypocrites, ye can discern the face of the sky; but can ye not discern the signs of the times?
⁴ A wicked and adulterous generation seeketh after a sign; and there shall no sign be given unto it, but the sign of the prophet Jonas. And he left them and departed.   ⁵ And when his disciples were come to the other side, they had forgotten to take bread.

[6] Then Jesus said unto them, Take heed and beware of the leaven of the Pharisees and of the Sadducees. [7] And they reasoned among themselves, saying, It is because we have taken no bread.   [8] Which when Jesus perceived, he said unto them, O ye of little faith, why reason ye among yourselves, because ye have brought no bread?

[9] Do ye not yet understand, neither remember the five loaves of the five thousand, and how many baskets ye took up?

[10] Neither the seven loaves of the four thousand, and how many baskets ye took up?   [11] How is it that ye do not understand that I spake it not to you concerning bread, that ye should beware of the leaven of the Pharisees and of the Sadducees?   [12] Then understood they how that he bade them not beware of the leaven of bread, but of the doctrine of the Pharisees and of the Sadducees.

Prophets Asleep To the Rise of Pure Evil
As a Christian growing up in America you would expect people would act in a certain moral manner which you could in some degree trust or rely upon. These days are now personal history in America where our culture and a nation is growing to reject Bible ethics and morality. In comparison many in the Charismatic Church has for a long time be taught a certain level of Christian takeover. In the Charismatic Prophetic Movement, a common practice has arisen to predict coming great national or international moves of God. Certain buzz words were

routinely spoken in order to convince the Charismatic Church about great coming revival. For decades Charismatics would hear from their prophets "break through is coming," or God is going to restore back what has been stolen or destroyed. Another prophetic buzz philosophy, God is going to give you a fresh anointing or mantle. So familiar has revival prophetic philosophy invaded the Charismatic Movement the prophets attached revival philosophy to the Trump Presidency.

Another favorite practice among the Charismatic prophets is to take events from sporting events, or other high-profile situations and spin a tale about how that event is a sign form God. For example, when Kanas City wins the Super Bowl, it is a sign from God a great revival will begin with its origin coming from Kanas City. Of course, not of any of these prophetic predictions has even come close to being what has been predicted. Then Charismatics like to play the game of unreality that somehow their prediction was fulfilled just not in the way expected.

With their prophetic model in place thousands of false prophecies have been given spanning over several decades. As predictions fall to the ground it exposes the fact the prophets are not hearing from God and are become a great source of deception error.

In 2020 all these methods were brought to a head with events which none of the prophets could have predicted. The prophetic model was exposed for what it has be doing for decades, but manly just ignored and covered up. What has happened to make the prophetic ministry so out of touch and false? Inside the prophetic camp there is no place for a deceived defeated Church. Inside the prophetic camp there is no room for the recognition of man's depravity and evil arising bringing absolute corruption. We could say the prophetic ministry has eliminated the doctrine of total depravity. As popular apostles teach the prophetic is all about bringing the gold out of a person. Anyone who embraces this philosophy has been tempted to associate the goodness of man present in every person on earth. This why the Prophetic Movement practices prophesying prophetic words of destiny over spiritually dead persons. However, the Bible teaches men born in sin are natural enemies to God and are by nature children of Gods wrath. The goodness of man philosophy cannot be found In Scriptures.

So, what happened in 2020? The prophets went on with predictive prophetic words as business should continue as usual. However, what has been covered up by failed predictions being pushed under the carpet and hidden below the surface for decades now came right out in the open. Instead of man's goodness, pure evil came into open view. What the prophets have refused to see is the rise of pure evil which will accompany the last days. The days of trying to manage the corruption of sin and death by the Church has come to a delusional end.

The wickedness which is arising in the earth will finally spread over the whole world in gross darkness. Even now evil men and imposters are waxing worse and worse being deceived and deceiving. Evil is on display with men and women in the government, the media, entertainment, and in the Church. Instead of the Church purifying cultural corruption wickedness is abounding and spreading abroad like a plague. Soon the world will be filled with antichrist beliefs, and pure evil will be celebrated from the four corners of the world.

In America men and women are always decreeing science to back up their evil practices. They are teaching our children God did not create them male and female. They want grade school children to be taught how to be sexually immoral. They want no boundaries to prevent their own sexual perversions and many already have given themselves to sex with children. They are cunning liars who tell you what you want to hear while they will not follow the very laws you are required to obey. The apostle Paul said he had wrestled with wild beasts of men, who are demonized and Satanic. Does the Charismatic prophetic ministry then pretend evil men, and pure evil will be tamed by the Church?

The wild beast is arising, the prophets want to proclaim a new era for the Church must close their eyes to the growth of pure evil. We live in a time where we are moving very quickly towards the Great Tribulation, and the worlds darkest hour. The prophets who have their heads in the clouds are asleep to the pure evil which is arising in the earth, and false prophecy which helps to prepare the coming of the worlds false Messiah. An evil so malevolent the world will openly worship Satan as God. A people so corrupt they will openly blasphemy Jesus Christ and make Christianity illegal on the whole earth.

Now are the prophets you are following preparing the Church for the coming Great Tribulation? The darkest days on earth that will ever exist from the creation of the world to the end of the present evil age.

2 Timothy 3
1 This know also, that in the
last days perilous times shall come.
2 For men shall be lovers of their own
selves, covetous, boasters, proud, blasphemers, disobed
ient to parents, unthankful, unholy,
3 Without natural affection, trucebreakers, false
accusers, incontinent, fierce, despisers of those that are
good,
4 Traitors, heady, high minded, lovers of
pleasures more than lovers of God;
5 Having a form of godliness, but denying the
power thereof: from such turn away.
6 For of this sort are they which
creep into houses, and lead captive silly
women laden with sins, led away with divers lusts,
7 Ever learning, and never able to come to the

knowledge of the truth.

8 Now as Jannes and Jambres withstood Moses, so do t
hese also resist the truth: men corrupt
minds, reprobate concerning the faith.

9 But they shall proceed no further: for their folly shall
be manifest unto all men, as theirs also was.

10 But thou hast fully known my doctrine, manner of
life, purpose, faith, longsuffering, charity, patience,

11 Persecutions, afflictions, which came unto
me at Antioch, at Iconium, at Lystra; what persecutions I
endured: but out of them all the Lord delivered me.

12 Yea, and all that will live godly in Christ Jesus shall
suffer persecution.

13 But evil men and seducers shall wax worse and
worse, deceiving, and being deceived.

14 But continue thou in the things which thou hast
learned and

Chapter Two
Failed Trump Prophecies

Charismatics Confusion and Anger

If you want to see the bad fruit of false prophetic
predictions over the Trump reelection, just look at all
the anger and confusion. Hardly can many talk with
peace when someone points out how all these last four
years of prophetic manipulation and presumption are
now nothing more than failed words of man.
Charismatics think you have compromised your faith if

you point out false predictions. Even now the narrative of a Trump victory is being pushed, to keep the carrot dangled out before those who will not give up on Trump's defeat. Why are Charismatics so angry with one another? Here is the truth, many who would not go along with the false prophetic predictions still voted for President Trump. Many die-hard Charismatics cannot get this out of their mind, it is one thing to expose corruption in the prophets, and another totally separate issue on voting for President Trump.

Take for example four years ago the false prediction President Trump was a modern-day King Cyrus who would by government lead the nation into revival. Now Charismatics can completely reject this false Gospel, and still stand in support of President Trump. Let us be clear, no one who is Christian would want America overthrown by sciolistic communism. Also, we know Christians are in support of the Pro-Life position and stand with Israel. All these things President Trump supported, as well as favoring the Christian faith. However, the false Gospel promoted by self-declared prophets were just jumping on the band wagon of the Trump Presidency to attain some measure of audience and credibility by exploiting the Presidency. In the end, Charismatics horribly failed President Trump by false prophetic word after false prophetic word. Imagine what President Trump might feel after all those lying prophetic predictions spoken in the name of the Lord.

The Charismatic prophets lifted up President Trump, setting him up for a huge fall.

Charismatic prophets have lacked godly integrity and wanted to be seen with President Trump. Even now a lack of Christ like character is being demonstrated, as the prophets continue to promote their ministries in the face of this horrible deception. Now we have thousands, if not millions of Charismatics running around seeking to justify why they followed false prophetic predictions. It is like a virus is spreading through the whole of the Charismatic Prophetic Movement, but hardly any have the character to stand up and put a stop to the plague. Perhaps the greatest evidence of those who claim to be prophets but are lacking in the fruit of authentic prophetic ministry, comes from their own self-preservation. First, they are guilty of speaking perversely in the name of the Lord and were not afraid of self-promotion. Now after being caught in their own deceit, are trying to save themselves from any consequences. How can any man or women who will not admit they have fallen to deception, be the Lord's prophets?

The divide among the deceived, and those who speak out against the false prophecy is clearly seen. It is sad when self-declared prophets speak of persecution and the lack of brotherly love when they have created the problem in the first place. They were so desperate to create a following, a platform for their ministries they compromised with the Lord. All the confusion and hate is the result of seducing the Church and creating a schism. Those who were seduced to follow prophetic voices with a false narrative ended up divided by prophetic schisms in the body of Christ. False prophetic predictions, and fantasy have seduced the Prophetic Movement into following personalities at the expense of being lead of the Holy Spirit. As the false prophetic has been a work of the flesh all along, the fruit is now the works of the flesh. Anger, hate, mistrust, unforgiveness, are being played out among Charismatics in a great division.

Let be clear, the false prophetic has made the Charismatic Movement sick. Those who have for years fed off the glorification of man, need to be confronted and held accountable. If any supposed prophet says they could not but help speak these failed predictions, then they were never in control. As the spirit of the prophets are subject to the prophets. None can say, "God made me say it." The pushed their own agenda to speak presumptuously in the name of the Lord. Not just one, instead the whole prophetic crowd got caught in the Satanic snare. Healing the division, and anger will only come as true admission of deception and error is openly confessed by high profile leaders. Both those inside the Movement and outside the Movement must now find the grace and humility to admit deep level deception and error in a true spirit of repentance. The wound in Charismatics must be brought out into the light and cleansed by the blood of Jesus Christ. Anything less, will end up in the growing fruit of apostasy and away from authentic revival desperately need in our day.

1 Corinthians 14:29-40

29 Let the prophets speak two or three, and let the other judge.

30 If anything be revealed to another that sitteth by, let the first hold his peace.

31 For ye may all prophesy one by one, that all may learn, and all may be comforted.

32 And the spirits of the prophets are subject to the prophets.

33 For God is not the author of confusion, but of peace, as in all churches of the saints.

34 Let your women keep silence in the churches: for it is not permitted unto them to speak; but they are commanded to be under obedience, as also saith the law.

35 And if they will learn anything, let them ask their husbands at home: for it is a shame for women to speak in the church.

36 What? came the word of God out from you? or came it unto you only?

37 If any man think himself to be a prophet, or spiritual, let him acknowledge that the things that I write unto you are the commandments of the Lord.

38 But if any man be ignorant, let him be ignorant.

39 Wherefore, brethren, covet to

prophesy, and forbid not to speak with tongues.
40 Let all things be done decently and in order.

Charismatic Prophets Must Do Some Deep Soul
Searching

The false prophecies of President Trump are now
coming to a head. The Charismatic prophets are doing a
lot of posturing. As they had proclaimed the Church
could know wither or not, they are true prophets by
their Trump predictions coming to past. However,
misguided that belief has been, their predictive words
were never the true measure of them being prophets or
not. It has only proven one thing with a shout from the
roof tops the Charismatic prophet ministry has been off
for years. To build a ministry around President Trump
and prophetic predictions was off from the very
beginning. A waste of time a complete misdirection, and
the worse of all a false witness of Jesus Christ. As I have
said before prophetic words over Donald Trump were
about a theological philosophy not true prophetic words
from Jesus Christ. Now time and time again prophetic
predictions were given to prove a false premise God
was raising up Donald Trump to save America. In short
God and government were being married in this
Charismatic philosophical belief. It has now come
crashing to the ground exposing all the vanity by false
predicting in the name of the Lord.

Let me ask the prophets a question? When did the prophetic ministry become about you? I know this for a fact God sent saints to your life to warn you of your excess and error. Initially, you were called of God and given gifts to support your prophetic calling. You have corrupted those graces by making the ministry about you, your prophetic predictions were about your fame, your ministry platforms, and money. Also worse of all " the man-made glory" by which you have surrounded your ministry so as to ignore all the danger of being lifted up in exaltation.

Here in lies the danger, these predictions are all about your calling as a prophet and were given in the name of the Lord. You have corrupted the testimony and witness of Jesus Christ by giving false prophecy. Then you excuse yourself as if all were words were based upon meeting certain conditions which you never stated until your predictions were proven false. Don't you see you lie about God's character and nature? As God is omniscient knowing the beginning from the end, God has always known about the results of the election. God has always fully seen and know all about how corruption in government would affect the Trump Presidency. God did not need your help to get President Trump elected by your prophetic predictions.

You might protest God gave you a dream or vision. To which I answer Gods words are infallible, and your susceptibility to deception is no excuse. I am a

Charismatic and have dreams and visions from time to time. Never have I thought any of those were infallible or treated in that manner. I was given a dream several weeks ago Donald Trump would simply fade away. I did not know what to really think as all other Charismatics were emphatic in their visions and trips to heaven Trump was to be reelected. Of course, the prophets have been given false prophecy for many years. However, Charismatics have been satisfied if supposed prophets get one out of ten right, as that one becomes the fanatic word in place for all the rest of their failed predictions. However, God did not think so. Now the world is mocking all the Charismatic pretense. The Charismatic Prophetic Movement has been guilty of being a false witness of Jesus Christ.

How grave is the danger to give failed predictions in the name of the Lord. Here are the words of Jesus Christ warning of the false prophets who lead the people into the broad way of destruction. Not everyone one who says to Me Lord Lord shall enter the Kingdom of Heaven but they who do the will of My Father in Heaven. For many will come to me on that day (the day of Judgement) and say Lord did we not prophesy in your name...? I will say to them depart from Me your workers of iniquity for I never knew you. As much as the prophets have prophesied falsely in the name of the Lord is their danger before the Judgment Seat of Christ.

They will attempt to excuse their false testimonies before the Lord, however all in vain. A false witness is in grave danger at the Judgement, their failed predictions bare witness they spoke vainly in the name of the Lord. All who excused themselves and have not truly repented of their false witness are in danger of being excluded from entrance into the Kingdom age. For your few scraps of human praise, you have sold your birth right to false predictions. Sad will be the day when you finally give an account before God. Or you can break before God in full disclosure you have been tempted and seduced wanting your ministry to be idolized. You can put your ministry on the alter and which God burn it up in judicial fire, so your soul can be saved on the Day of the Lord. God hates a false witness did you think somehow God is excusing your lies in the name of your prophetic reputation.

1 Corinthians 3:7-23
7 So then neither is he that
planteth anything, neither he that
watereth; but God that giveth the increase.
8 Now he that planteth and he
that watereth are one: and every man shall receive his
own reward according to his own labour.
9 For we are labourers together with God: ye
are God's husbandry, ye are God's building.
10 According to the grace of God which is given unto
me, as a wise master builder, I have laid the
foundation, and another buildeth thereon. But let every

man take heed how he buildeth thereupon.

11 For other foundation can no man lay than that is laid, which is Jesus Christ.

12 Now if any man build upon this foundation gold, silver, precious stones, wood, hay, stubble;

13 Every man's work shall be made manifest: for the day shall declare it, because it shall be revealed by fire; and the fire shall try every man's work of what sort it is.

14 If any man's work abide which he hath built thereupon, he shall receive a reward.

15 If any man's work shall be burned, he shall suffer loss: but he himself shall be saved; yet so as by fire.

16 Know ye not that ye are the temple of God, and that the Spirit of God dwelleth in you?

17 If any man defile the temple of God, him shall God destroy; for the temple of God is holy, which temple ye are.

18 Let no man deceive himself. If any man among you seemeth to be wise in this world, let him become a fool, that he may be wise.

19 For the wisdom of this world is foolishness with God. For it is written, He taketh the wise in their own craftiness.

20 And again, The Lord knoweth the thoughts of the wise, that they are vain.

21 Therefore let no man glory in men. For all things are yours;

22 Whether Paul, or Apollos, or Cephas, or the

world, or life, or death, or things present, or things to come; all are yours;
23 And ye are Christ's; and Christ is God's.

Do Charismatics Really Know What Went Wrong?

I have noticed some of the prophets begin to admit the bad fruit they have produced by giving false prophetic predictions. I find it interesting after leading thousands of Charismatics into false beliefs and practices, the prophets are now shocked and alarmed by their kick back. Many Charismatics simply have fallen into a radicalized position and are rebuking the prophets for their repentance. Here is what is really funny, and sad, when the prophets proclaim the Movement which they have created is "sick." Can the prophets who misguided the Charismatics for the last four years writing books and producing dozens of videos now act "surprised at the deprivation which they have created?" The let us get over its attitude, and admittance of wrongdoing, but let us move on with my ministry is alarming. Let us get real they have sowed a false Gospel for many years now the bad fruit has come to maturity.

Here is the next danger. When prophets who were blind and leading others into blindness attempt to say, "I see what I did wrong." Here is one prophet's methodology: I went to my elders to be held accountable. Next, I am a member of a local Church, so I am a man under authority not a rogue prophet. Here is the problem with these statements? First the prophets was already in relationship with those same elders, likely other apostles/prophets who are blinded by the same beliefs and practices. When the false predictions were given those very elders were already supportive and blinded to the same deceptions. Next when we see a prophet say I am a member of a local Church, that Church likely has had little to none say in directing the prophet's ministry. Who would ever allow their multi millions dollars ministries to be shut down because of being corrected for false ministry? It just does not happen in our day. Most of what men say when pointing to being under authority, really means their friends in ministry are supportive. Usually, little to no action of corruption or discipline results like stepping down from ministry at least for a season. Usually with a public apology, the show will just go on.

Now here is something really shallow. When self-declared prophets begin to correct their own blindness. Charismatics are now in a time after several decades where high profile apostles/prophets are attempting to confront the blindness which they have walked in for years. It almost comical to watch supposed apostles/prophets "talk about false prophets and false practices." While they are some of the major sources of those very things. For years they have been called out by Christians both inside and outside the Prophetic

Movement for being "false prophets." It has become comical when those charged as false prophets, are attempting to expose false prophets. They have been called on the carpet, and now are acting all spiritual about the manner as if they are being guided by integrity.

False prophets, those who got it wrong for years have been blind, You cannot now say "I see," just so you appease those who approve of your ministry. Here is the facts:) 1 You have been blind to the truth.) 2 You have given false witness) 3 You have not been led of the Holy Spirit, but thought you were)4 You were in the flesh, and exalted in self-will) 5 When God warned you about deception outside your support base, you pushed it off)6 Your false doctrine, and philosophies have brought you into dangerous waters of ship wreck) Many Christians you seduced with false prophetic ministry, will fall away from the Lord)7 You are still blind, as years of false doctrines and philosophies have established personal beliefs which are completely false.)8 Those who saw your blindness saw how you exalted your false doctrines and philosophies over the doctrines of Jesus Christ.

For all the false apostles/prophets whose false doctrine blinded you, and millions of other Charismatics it is time to be exposed for your false Gospel. Until true exposure of these doctrines and philosophies happens, the whole prophetic Movement will continue under deception.

False prophets cannot correct other false prophets. Neither can they see the fulness of their own blindness and deception.

Two Big Lies By Prophetic

Right now, the Charismatic Movement needs a deep level reckoning about all the falsehood coming out of the prophetic ministry. 2020 has exposed how the Charismatic prophets are blinded and are in danger of misleading the Church. Let us face it, no supposed prophet rightly predicted the events of 2020. The complete opposite has been happening in comparison to what they predicted. Now as 2021 rolls around the predictive words are already beginning to roll out as if nothing has happened and the show must go on. Without a deep level exposure of corruption inside the prophetic ministry, no one should give credence to the character and accountability of the Prophetic Movement.

Here a two dangerous areas which are current deceptions within the Movement. QAnon, a conspiracy theory has been adopted into the prophetic. The main propagator of QAnon as a predictive word of prophecy is the 7 Mountain Kingdom Now prophets. They have fixated on President Trump as an agent secretly working inside government exposing the deep state. Also, Trump is being used by God to expose the high-profile pedophile ring which they say involves all manner of celebrities like Oprah, Tom Hanks, and Hillary. QAnon has captured the imagination of Christians with secret messages given by code which reveal plans to expose all this deep state, and celebrity corruption. Several well know prophets of the 7 Mountain Kingdom Now worldwide Church take over has blended the 7 Mountain philosophy with QAnon to direct Charismatics through QAnon predictions.

So serious is the conspiracy deceptions coming through one Charismatic QAnon prophet his own daughter began to expose her father's spiritual blindness. How little does the Charismatic Movement see the danger of allowing a platform for false prophets through sources like Charisma Magazine, and The Elijah List to spread the QAnon deception. Those who stand outside the QAnon conspiracy influences see the Prophetic Movement as a right-wing political cult like following of President Trump. How deep the deception when the 7 Mountain Prophetic Movement heralded President Trump as a modern-day King Cyrus. From there major prophetic voices began to build a whole prophetic philosophy around President Trump. The Seven Mountain Prophetic Movement wrote all manner of books which described how God has raised up Trump a modern-day deliverer to lead the nation into revival. So great has been this 7 Mountain philosophy all the prophets predicted a landslide reelection. So convinced were the Trump prophets, one made a blanket statement if the all the prophets falsely predicted a Trump reelection, then there was a major problem in the Charismatic Prophetic Movement.

The Second big lie has already started inside the Prophetic Movement. Despite all the exposure of deep level corruption going on in America, the prophet's yearly prediction declare there will be "a new era," not just a new season or new day, a new era. The philosophy which drives the Prophetic Movement does not allow for any manner of a great apostasy, or a defeated Church of any kind. Almost 100% of the Charismatic prophets are looking for a great revival, a worldwide Church take over. The prophets reject the idea of a coming Great Tribulation, a coming Antichrist, and a Great Falling Away from the faith.

Here is the Great danger in predicting a new era, a time of worldwide rule and conversion by the Church. A Golden age upon the earth, a utopian like Kingdom upon the earth. Where the Church has spread the Kingdom of heaven all over the world before Jesus Christ can return. These philosophical beliefs have created a great blindness inside the Prophetic Movement. As none of these beliefs can actually been seen in real life, false and lying predictions are utilized to mislead Charismatics in this philosophical beliefs. Sadly, a new era is coming and even now we see its signs. The new era is not what Charismatics are prophetically predicting. Instead, it is the coming time of the world's greatest trial ever. A time identified by the Scriptures as the Great Tribulation which occurs before the return of the Lord. Ironically, the false predictions coming from the Charismatic prophets is deceiving the Church into accepting the coming Antichrist. The exact 100% opposite is happening, not a new era a golden age of Charismatics, instead a new era of the Antichrist and Great Tribulation.

The Prophets are blind guides who cannot see the truth and who lack the integrity to expose their own deception. How can any Christian put their confidence in Charismatic prophets? You are subjecting yourself to a spirit of error, which the Bible teaches is the antichrist spirit.

1 John 4:1-6

1 Beloved, believe not every spirit, but try the spirits whether they are of God: because many false prophets are gone out into the world.

2 Hereby know ye the Spirit of God: Every spirit that confesseth that Jesus Christ is come in the flesh is of God:

3 And every spirit that confesseth not that
Jesus Christ is come in the flesh is not of God: and this is
that spirit of antichrist, whereof ye have heard that it
should come; and even now already is it in the world.
4 Ye are of God, little children, and have
overcome them: because greater is he that is
in you, than he that is in the world.
5 They are of the world: therefore speak they of the
world, and the world heareth them.
6 We are of God: he that knoweth God heareth us; he
that is not of God heareth not us. Hereby know we the
spirit of truth, and the spirit of error.

Dominion Theology Failed Charismatics

The Cross is the Gospel of the Scriptures. The preaching
of the Cross is the power of God unto salvation for
those who believe. Unto the perishing the Cross is
foolishness. The temptation then is to improve upon the
message of the Cross to make it more attractive in the
eyes of mankind. When we add to the Cross or take
away a false Gospel then is created which creates great
deception in the Church. The apostle Paul warned about
false apostles who preached another Gospel, and
brought in a false Jesus, and did so by another spirit
other than the Holy Spirit. Today we have many self-
proclaimed apostles and prophets who preach a false
Gospel called Dominion Theology. Right now,
Charismatic Dominion Theology is exposed by its false
prediction of a worldwide Church reformation and

revival. Dominion Theology led to the prophets failed predictions attempting to bring revival through the Trump Presidency, and it has fallen to the ground bringing great reproach to the Lord.

Now these apostles and prophets will insist they are orthodox and preach the Cross. However, theirs is a false twisting of Scriptures which gives a dominion to the Church which God never gave. The Charismatics insist the Cross has restored to the Church dominion which Adam lost in the Garden. From a false restored dominion, the Charismatics then set out to subdue the world and rule over it. The Charismatics have called this false Gospel the Dominion Mandate to rule over the world they way God commissioned Adam to rule over the Garden. With the Dominion Mandate in hand the Charismatics teach the Church is in the Kingdom Now and can restore Garden like conditions to the earth before Jesus Christ can return.

Of course, God did not give restored Adamic dominion to the Charismatics, so they attempt to bring credibility to their false Gospel by using false prophetic predictions. As what they say in the name of the Lord is not actually a prophetic word, instead a doctrinal statement of Dominion Theology using a prophetic model to attract the Charismatics to their false Gospel.

For decades, the apostles and prophets have preached their dominionism through false prophecy, and the treating it as it were a true prophetic utterance given by the Lord. Thousands of false prophecies have been compiled and marketed over several decades by the apostles and prophets. Making this the single largest aberrant Charismatic Movement in Church history. Leading millions of Charismatics into a false Gospel, which has gotten so far out of hand the Movement is in gross danger of leading millions into apostasy. The sheer amount of false prediction and commitment to New Age practices demonstrates the absolute abandonment by the Movement from the Foundation of the Christian faith, the message of the Cross.

Now the house of cards is come crashing down as Dominion Theology has failed to produce the Trump revival which was so often promoted by the prophets in the last four years. Of course, the apostles and prophets inside the Movement are downplaying the seriousness of the failed predictions. Charismatics must remember these are the very same prophets who wrote books on the Trump revolution. Instead of one failed Presidential prediction this is the false Gospel which has seduced Charismatics for years. Any Christian who wants to make light of the false prophets who carry false prophecy and have promoted a failed False Gospel are just inviting the church into shipwreck.

Many Charismatics will have not understood how they have been taught to exchange the Gospel of Salvation for Dominion Theology. The most common name by which Dominion Theology is promoted by apostles and prophets is called the 7 Mountain Mandate. The basic philosophy of the 7 Mountain Gospel is the Charismatic Church will cleanse the seven pillars of culture making for Christian cities and nations before Jesus Christ can return. As there is no single shred of evidence the Charismatics have even one inch of ability to Christianize the world. So then to legitimate their false Gospel, Charismatic prophets affixed the Seven Mountain Dominionism upon the Trump Presidency. The prophets then declared President Trump a modern-day King Cyrus who would cleanse the pillar of government and bring revival to the United States. Now that Trump was not re-elected the Charismatic Church is in an uproar, with all manner of delusion, hate and anger. The 7 Mountain Gospel has brought great division to the body of Christ and has produced a great number of false messengers who the Charismatics believe are apostles and prophets. In truth the Seven Mountain Charismatic Movement has divided the body of Christ, making for Christians to choose men over the Lordship of Jesu Christ. Christians idolizing and glorifying men who have drawn them away from the Lord and unto themselves to make disciples after own image. To make a personal profit off the Church by gaining glorification from man and their devotion and riches. The whole Seven Mountain Movement has been corrupted by this manner of bad fruit, and to this point is highly exalted by man to make it without correction.

Angels Who Reveal Our Next President

Lately it has been popular for Charismatics who are prophetic to say angels have told them Donald Trump is to be re-elected as our next President. One such supposed prophetic woman said she saw a thousand angels in heaven wearing red, white, and blue, political garments who were sent to help Donald Trump be the next President. Why are Charismatics going to such lengths to say angels are controlling the next election? First of all, I completely reject this woman's version of prophetic ministry, and communication with angels. She is the same person who said she can go into heaven upon demand, and saw in heaven a Jell-O room for kids, and Disneyland like roller coasters. Yet, tens of thousands of Charismatics faithfully follow her vein imaginations into a fantasy world of lying visions, and dark angels who are transforming for her into angels of light. Why would any Christian validate such nonsense is beyond me? The closest thing I place such individuals who give such falsehood is to be demonized, and or mentally ill. Why would any Christian think these are visions or angelic communication from God?

Still other supposed Charismatic prophets speak of angels like Gabriel telling them President Trump was to be elected. Why so much angelic communication coming out of the Charismatics? First of all, in the election only one of two candidates will be elected our next President. So, predicting the next President statically speaking is not any big mystery. When you say God told me, or an angel showed me, you are saying heaven is behind the election of one of the candidates. So, you are saying God stands behind President Trump as His chosen one. What is unique about God's ability is His infallibility, if God wants it to happen it cannot fail. Yet we see with Charismatics false predictions all the time where they give political future forecasts, and then they are false. Some kind of supposed revelation from God which exalts one candidates' future, and yet it fails to happen as they have predicted. Why are angels and political predictions become such an emphasis among Charismatics?

Does God know who is going to be the next President? Yes, He does. Will God then stand for the next President as His choice. Absolutely yes. What then is the problem? The assumption Charismatics have made that all is well with Gods appointed man for President. Let us get this straight, whoever is chosen to be the next President, will have to face an America which has turned its back on God. No angel, no prophet, no President can make America great again unless we turn from our national sin. The false assumption is the next President will save America is completely wrong. America's slide away from God has brought a divided nation of hate, racism, murder, and lawlessness. Do you think America is going to go back to better days of Gods favor and blessing by electing a certain President? Many Charismatics proclaimed the first Trump Presidency, and we have seen four years of a demonic America. Not that Trump is to blame, it is the sin and love of darkness America has fallen into. When a Charismatic says an angel showed me, or God told me, it then is assumed all is well for the next four years. This is a false presumption; America's next four years will likely be some of the greatest turmoil any one of us has ever lived in this nation. The next President has inherited a demonically divided nation and increasing darkness through situations like modern day plagues.

Let us stop the Charismatic games, the fantasy of Charismatics which are out of control. Let us get real all the false predictions of 2020 is a sham and proof angels and prophecy cannot fix the deep darkness America has fallen into. America Christians need to see the days we live in are full of the antichrist spirit. Satan is active in this nation with all manner of evil including dark fallen angels who are giving false lying visions. The prophets of the Charismatic Movement are being sold a bill of goods; their philosophy cannot save the world. Now angels have become a big part of their philosophical practice. When America has fallen, they say angels show them America's future is bright. Charismatics say angels of revival will bring the nation back to God again. No matter the current state of evil, Charismatics say an angel will change it. I want to say they are caught in Satanic deception with dark Angels seducing them.

What will happen? America is being warned by God Himself. Evil men and imposters are waxing worse and worse deceiving and being deceived. Perilous times are upon us as wicked and evil rulers are being elected to bring the nation under greater darkness. I believe perverse rulers are the result of America turning its back on God. The Church must stand up in repentance and find its way back to God from fake Christianity. When the Church recovers the Gospel Message once again and preaches the Cross of Jesus Christ as the only way to save this nation. Then all the prophecies and angelic communication of our next President having to save the nation will have no place. As our Savior will be Jesus Christ alone, and no other man, or host of angels. The is no other name under heaven by which a man can be saved. Jesus Christ is that name and must be found in the mouths of the Church once again.

Charismatics Correcting the Charismatic Movement

In the last couple of years, a great outcry has arisen concerning the deception which has dominated the Prophetic Charismatic Movement. A lot of the confrontation has come from Evangelicals who are outside of the Charismatic experience. I must embrace the integrity I have experienced coming from Evangelicals who have upheld the authority of the Written Word of God. The Biblical principles held by Evangelicals has been in many cases the guide which has keep them falling into deception and error. On the other hand, Charismatics have often been very loose concerning doctrine, willing to let subject revelations have more authority than the Written Word of God. The temptation to undermine the authority of Scriptures as a practice in the whole Prophetic Movement, has been exemplified by the rewriting of Scriptures to fit with Kingdom Now philosophy as was done in the Passion Translation Bible. The official Bible of the apostolic/prophetic leaders, of the who is who in the Movement.

I have come out from the Prophetic Movement and have been an outspoken voice of concern, asking for more accountability in the Movement. Over many years I have seen a shift inside the Movement, with more Charismatics separating themselves no longer being able to abide in the teachings and practices. Lately, a growing awaking Of Charismatics willing to speak up and speak out to join a every growing shout of alarm. Now with another high visible Charismatic leader being exposed in sexual immorality, a great divide seems to be happening among Charismatics. Simply put many Charismatic's can no longer abide in a Movement which has gone away from the centrality of Jesus Christ. This signals a shift, of voices which have formerly directed and influenced the Movement. As the former generation of leaders could not confront, or correct the deception and errors, new leaders are arising who have the ability. Many of these new leaders are sovereignly chosen by God, who are just emerging, and will lead the Millennial generation of Charismatic's.

I want to speak as a Charismatic Christian and to our Evangelical brothers in Christ. There is a great difference in opinion as how to respond to false apostles, prophets, and teachers inside the Prophetic Movement. I know for certain we must expose any heretical teaching and teachers. Also, a great number of false prophets, who are exposed as predators exploiting other Christians. Some have even met the qualifications of wolf like character and are being called out as wolves in sheep's clothing. As this time is very difficult and dangerous many Christians must warn others. I have spent many hundreds of hours and articles doing this very thing. So, sympathize with the strong warnings, and voice of alarm, even the debates on the internet. So here in lies the problem, in the midst of confrontation and correction can come sin and flesh. As God is acting to confront many serious concerns, we watch over our own hearts as our attitudes and words reveal our own weakness and flesh.

On my part, I have never been comfortable with the titles or labels of "wolf or false brother, or emissary of Satan." I will tell you why, I have in some cases meet these men personally, have seen their rise into falsehood before there were famous in the Charismatic Movement. I have never felt these men did not have the born-again experience, even though now many would doubt they had ever been saved. So, I do not want to give a false testimony as if their behaviors now mean they were never saved in the first place. Your theology might not have a grid for apostate teachers, being deceived brothers in Christ. You might be comfortable labeling a man or woman who is obviously a false prophet, an emissary of Satan. However, I agree a born-again man can fall into the snare of the devil and teach doctrines of demons. If I have known them as brothers in Christ, shall I now declare they "were never saved?" I simply do not carry that theology, and I stand by my words of confrontation as "I must give an account of every word spoken," at the Judgment Seat of Christ.

Here is my position, A false prophet can be a brother in Christ which has fallen into being a predator, a false prophet. Many Charismatics have already acted in great wickedness, preying upon the Church in a wolf like way, absolutely. Should a famous false prophet receive excommunication from the Church if he does not repent, most definitely. I look for his or repentance and laying down of their ministry before they stand before the Lord. Are Charismatic false prophets dangerous to the Church, absolutely. Should false prophets be marked and avoided, absolutely it is the only reasonable and righteous thing to do. Will I reject false prophets as a brother in Christ, the answer is no. I must pray and ask God to act, even if God's action is a matter of life and death. For this cause, many are weak and sick and have died prematurely. However, I will not sin by falling in the error of hating my brother in Christ for his gross sin and error. Please understand I am making judgment on sin, and deception, but I cannot make the saving blood of Jesus Christ any less for my brother in Christ. May God judge in mercy so his soul may be saved in the Day of the Lord.

1 Corinthians 10:23-34

23 For I have received of the Lord that which also I delivered unto you, That the Lord Jesus the same night in which he was betrayed took bread:

24 And when he had given thanks, he break it, and said, Take, eat: this is my body, which is broken for you: this do in remembrance of me.

25 After the same manner also he took the cup, when he had supped, saying, This cup is the new testament in my blood: this do ye, as oft as ye drink it, in remembrance of me.

26 For as often as ye eat this bread, and drink this cup, ye do shew the Lord's death till he come.

27 Wherefore whosoever shall eat this bread, and drink this cup of the Lord, unworthily, shall be guilty of the body and blood of the Lord.

28 But let a man examine himself, and so let him eat of that bread, and drink of that cup.

29 For he that eateth and drinketh unworthily, eateth and drinketh damnation to himself, not discerning the Lord's body.

30 For this cause, many are weak and sickly among you, and many sleep.

31 For if we would judge ourselves, we should not be judged.

32 But when we are judged, we are chastened of the Lord, that we should not be condemned with the world.

33 Wherefore, my brethren, when ye come together to eat, tarry one for another.

34 And if any man hunger, let him eat at home; that ye come not together unto condemnation. And the rest will I set in order when I come.

Chapter Three
Who Are Gods Prophets

Can A Christian Be A False Prophet

A formal statement has been drawn up by Charismatic leaders and company of apostles and prophets over the issue of the false Trump prophecies. As good as many portions of this statement are, I believe it to miss many of the main reasons the false prophecies happened in the first place. One of the main beliefs of their statement is a false prophet cannot be a "true born again Christian." However, Scriptures recognize many situations of sin and the work of the flesh which do in fact come from born again Christians. The apostle Paul gives a list which includes Adultery, hatred, sedition's, and heresies. Paul goes on to say the peril of the last days is men will preach and teach Christian tales and philosophy while denying the doctrines of Jesus Christ.

Also in Scriptures, from the first century Paul wrote of false apostles who had invaded the Church with a false Gospel, another Jesus, and another spirit. While the apostle John wrote of false prophets which had already invaded the Church.

Here is my concern with the Dr. Brown statement. While it addresses the problem of false prophecy, it ignores the false Gospel behind it, and the false apostolic and prophet ministries which promote it. There solution seems to have ignored the deeper warning that false prophets were in their midst. Also, the peril of false doctrines which lead the Church away from Jesus Christ unto another Jesus was not even in their radar.

Why such a simplistic approach, which seems to have overlooked the deeper issues in their midst? The answer lies in the high profile offenders which were present in signing the document. How is it a signer of the document which teaches the doctrines of the 7 Mountain Gospel, and has prophesied hundreds of false worldwide Church takeovers, and international revivals can be genuine? As none of their prophetic words have come to pass. What of the apostles who teach on New Age practices, like portals into heaven, Christian tarot cards, spirit travel, and say the Church is recovering from the New Age what was stolen? It is obvious many of the signers of this document are the greatest deceivers in the Charismatic Movement today.

Are they about to renounces their whole ministries, after decades of conferences, and book writings of teaching these false doctrines and New Age practices? I think not. As they are completely accepted in false doctrine leading the Church into deception, they are not considered false prophets or false apostles. While the New Testament clearly defines such workers of iniquity as deceivers. Can a man or women who is born again constantly teach false doctrine, and give false prophetic words be a true prophet of God? The answer is obvious, by their own definitions they are a deceitful worker. No apostle or prophet of God deceives the Church.

With so many deceivers in their midst, has no mention or room has been made for anyone being a false prophet? It seems the possibility has been completely eliminated by their doctrinal statement. Perhaps the greatest danger of the whole statement is the belief none of them who led the Charismatic Movement astray, is in danger of being exposed. Instead, their ministries are being preserved and validated. For what reason? The measure of their false doctrines and false prophecies? No. The fact they are born again, and are popular voices inside the Movement. Here is the irony. The Prophetic Movement which has generated thousands of false prophecies for decades. Has no false prophets or false apostles among them? Does this seem deceptive to anyone?

Here is a portion of their statement:

WE THEREFORE RECOGNIZE distinctions between a believer who gives an inaccurate prophecy (in which case they should acknowledge their error), a believer who consistently prophesies inaccurately (in which case we recognize that this person is not a prophet, and we urge them to stop prophesying), and a false prophet (whom we recognize as a false believer, a lost soul, calling them to repent and be saved).

2 Peter 2:15-2
15 Which have forsaken the right way, and are gone astray, following the way of Balaam the son of Bosor, who loved the wages of unrighteousness;
16 But was rebuked for his iniquity: the dumb ass speaki ng with man's voice forbad the madness of the prophet.
17 These are wells without water, clouds that are carried with a tempest; to whom the mist of darkness is reserved for ever.
18 For when they speak great swelling words of vanity, they allure through the lusts of the flesh, through much wantonness, those that were clean escaped from them who live in error.
19 While they promise them liberty, they themselves are the servants of corruption: for of whom a man is overcome, of the same is he brought in

bondage.

20 For if after they have escaped the pollutions of the world through the knowledge of the Lord and Saviour Jesus Christ, they
are again entangled therein, and overcome, the latter end is worse with them than the beginning.
21 For it had been better for them not to have known the way of righteousness, than, after they have known it, to
turn from the holy commandment delivered unto them.
22 But it is happened unto them according to the true proverb, The dog is turned to his own vomit again; and the sow that was washed to her wallowing in the mire.

Corrupted Fruit

Perhaps the Church is having difficulty seeing the kind of harvest which is being produced today. As the Scriptures warn of a corrupted harvest, the Church needs to be vigilant in testing the fruit. It is one of Satan's master plans to sow corrupted seed right in with the good seed, so the corrupted fruit grows up right alongside of the good fruit. The Parable of the Wheat and Tares reveals this kind of spiritual warfare, which exists right inside the Church. Satan began to sow the corrupted seed with false apostles and prophets right in the very beginning of the first century Church. Today's Church often acts like it is an offense against God to expose ministers who are sowing corrupted seeds, and who produce a corrupted harvest. All kinds of rules and boundaries have been set in place to "protect a corrupted minster."

According to Jesus how is one to detect a false prophet? The problem exists when you follow the prophets' signs and wonders, without testing the seed he is sowing. The prophet's ministry by its very nature is based upon supernatural power, especially in revelatory gifting. However, the prophet is held in check by the Written Word of God and cannot move outside of the boundary of what has already been written. The prophet does not have any seed coming from himself, instead the incorruptible seed which the prophet must sow only comes from God's Written Word. The incorruptible seed is the Word of God which lives and abides forever. The Gospel was already determined before the formation of the world, as Jesus Christ is the Lamb of God slain before the foundation of the world. Gods Gospel is eternal, the incorruptible seed produces the harvest of "born again sons and daughters."

The corrupted seed is the "false gospel," it is a mixture of "half-truths," looks like the authentic Gospel but produces a corrupted fruit. The fruit which has been corrupted looks good on the outside, but on the inside upon greater examination it is rotten to the core. Jesus Christ did not say there would be "no fruit," instead he said the fruit produced would be corrupted evil fruit. Popularity, and success by the world's standards, large crowds, with abundant speaking platforms are not the measure of a God given harvest. The seed sown, "the Gospel message," the incorruptible seed, the preaching of the Cross, Jesus Christ and Him crucified is the message which is the unadulterated Gospel.

Not what is the problem with famous high visible preachers today. They cannot be rich and famous; they cannot have big crowds by preaching the Cross. So, they have gone to another Gospel, to put it bluntly the have gone to Satan's Gospel. The men sowing it look charming, funny, gifted in speaking, can draw big audiences. However, the seed sown is another gospel, which makes them false apostles and prophets. The harvest they say is so great is corrupted seed, a counterfeit, doctrines of demons. In the end it will produce a harvest of wickedness the worst being counterfeited sons and daughters, who think they are following God, but have rottenness in their lives. Today we are experiencing the maturing harvest of wheat and tares, both are beginning to put on the full head of grain or weeds.

Do not think it strange by the acceleration of corrupted bad fruit. Also, the abundance of false prophets who are demonically inspired to preach doctrines of demons. Neither be dismayed by a counterfeit harvest of corrupted fruit which is being celebrated by false prophets and false revival, as the work of the Holy Spirit. Only heed the warning of apostasy and deception, as in the last days many shall depart from the faith having itching ears and will follow the wickedness of evil men and imposters. Who will wax worse and worse deceiving and being deceived? The apostles and prophets will be especially tempting as they will have an element of the supernatural in their ministries. However, the test will be actually simple; do they preach Jesus Christ and Him crucified? Does their message always reveal the Cross and person of Jesus Christ? Or do they preach mixture, a corrupted gospel, a corrupted seed. As no man can preach a corrupted false gospel and produce anything but corrupted bad fruit.

Deuteronomy 22:9
9 Thou shalt not sow thy vineyard with divers' seeds: lest the fruit of thy seed which thou hast sown, and the fruit of thy vineyard, be defiled.

1 Peter 1:23
23 Being born again, not of corruptible seed, but of incorruptible, by the word of God, which liveth and abideth forever.

Matthew 12:33-34
33 Either make the tree good, and his fruit good; or else make the tree corrupt, and his fruit corrupt: for the tree is known by his fruit.

34 O generation of vipers, how can ye, being evil, speak good things? for out of the abundance of the heart the mouth speaketh.

Matthew 7:15-20
15 Beware of false prophets, which come to you in sheep's clothing, but inwardly they are ravening wolves.
16 Ye shall know them by their fruits. Do men gather grapes of thorns, or figs of thistles?
17 Even so every good tree bringeth forth good fruit; but a corrupt tree bringeth forth evil fruit.
18 A good tree cannot bring forth evil fruit, neither can a corrupt tree bring forth good fruit.
19 Every tree that bringeth not forth good fruit is hewn down and cast into the fire.
20 Wherefore by their fruits ye shall know them.

Prophets Beginning To Admit Rotten Fruit

For years self-declared prophets have ignored the pleas from the body of Christ how corrupt the prophetic ministry had become. The main points of corruption were 1) personal and subjective revelations, private interpretations were being exalted over the written Word of God. 2) New Testament prophets were being treated by Charismatics as if their prophetic words carried the same wight of authority, as the written infallible Word of God. 3) The prophets (apostles too) were being lifted by the Charismatic Movement into an unnatural position, even being idolized by Charismatic followers 4) The prophets objected to their predictive prophetic words being judged and rejected. The common defense was to warn not to touch Gods anointed prophets or you would be judged by God. 5) Failed prophetic words were swept under the carpet, and the prophets who gave them continued as if nothing happened. 6) Platforms which promoted prophetic words did not expose false prophecy. 6) False doctrines, and philosophy were put into prophetic words creating a Schism, a heresy, a divided body. 7) If you exposed the prophetic heresy you were accused as a troublemaker and excluded from the prophetic/apostolic camp. A true division over false prophecy and a blind loyalty to prophets. 8) An extra Biblical Movement which took the 7 Mountain philosophy and targeted President Trump as its evidence. 9) All who rejected these teachings and practices were not part of the Movement, and disobeyed God by not following the prophets. You were considered not as spiritual and would be kept out of the next move of God and the coming great revival.

Now after four years of continual assault upon the body of Christ pushing the Trump revival, the self-declared prophets were backed into the corner by failed predictions. Public confessions began to be made by the same prophets, and in the beginning, they were championed as having integrity by some Charismatics. However, after brief applause the failed prophets came under a great assault of Charismatics which had taken their prophetic words to an extent which borders on insanity. Suddenly the popular prophets were charged with evil motives and unbelief. In some cases, death threats came from some in the Prophetic Movement against the prophet or their families. It has come to a point where the prophets are losing their support base, and mass following. All this has served as an awakening by their own admission "May have created this idol monster."

What is really happening with the prophets? They are being rebuked in an off handed way. They are being forced to see the rotten fruit Jesus Christ has warned with false prophets. Rotten fruit coming from prophetic error and deception, now coming to a head in the Charismatic Movement where Trump has become an idol to save a nation. The pride and exaltation of the prophets has come with a price, the people lifted up and now they are willing to crucify. The prophets fed off any measure of popularity and profit and considered this approval as God's approval. It has been one of the true weakness of modern prophets who say the serve God, but their fruit has been found in the approval of man. Now that they have confessed sin, the whole Movement must follow. Sadly, many Charismatics have swallowed the false prophetic hook line and sinker and are become radicalized into Trumpism.

What continues to be totally crazy are the numbers of
self-declared prophets who are still holding out Trump
will be inaugurated once again. The prophetic divide
runs deep into the Church a tremendous deception all
built upon false prophecy promoted to a level of
infallibility. Which may of the failed prophets are now
seeing and admitting has happened. The suffering by
rejection from the crazed mob is the rotten fruit of their
own doing. They sowed deception and now are reaping
destruction. The prophetic Movement is in danger of
caving in upon itself, resulting in many Christians
abandoning the Church and the Lord in total
disillusionment.

It is time for these prophets to greatly humble
themselves and in no fashion present themselves as
innocent victims being wrongly persecuted. Instead,
their repentance needs to demand total reform and
accountability inside the Charismatic Movement.
Correction and discipline needs to be real with real
confessions of deception and leading the Church into
error. Even if it would cost them their ministries and
they have come to known they could no longer depend
on monies coming from a support base. How dire is the
warning in Scriptures for those who deceive the Church,
and lead schisms bringing division into the body of
Christ? Repentance is the only thing which will stop the
reaping of destruction which Christ has warned. God is
not mocked if a man who is called prophet has sown

according to the flesh, from the flesh he will reap destruction. Prophets wake up you are being called to give an account and are guilty of false testimony speaking in the name of the Lord. How dangerous to speak presumptuously in the name of the Lord. So did the false prophets which were before you. Their damnation does not stand afar off.

2 Peter 2:1-3

1 But there were false prophets also among the people, even as there shall be false teachers among you, who privily shall bring
in damnable heresies, even denying the Lord that bought them, and bring
upon themselves swift destruction.
2 And many shall follow their pernicious ways; by reason of whom the way of truth shall be evil spoken of.
3 And through covetousness shall they with feigned words make merchandise of you: whose judgment now of a long
time lingereth not, and their damnation slumbereth not.

The Danger of Following Balaam the False Prophet

Today in the modern Charismatic Movement is the presence of false prophets. The kind of false prophets which fall into the category of being like Balaam, the madness of the prophet which God rebuked by Balaam's own donkey.

What are some of the characteristics we must watch for in modern day Balaam like false prophet.?

1) They walk after the flesh without the fear of the Lord. They have the lust of uncleanness, having eyes of adultery, cannot cease from sin. Use their ministries of prophetic to beguile unstable souls inside the Church.

2) They are presumptuous, self-entitled, self-willed, and are a law unto themselves. Which means when they commit adultery and walk in perversity, they imagine themselves above the law and without correction. When confronted with their immoral behaviors are not afraid to rail against God's government, refusing to be corrected.

3) They count it a pleasure to live immorally right in the middle of the Church, and the love feasts of the Lord. They are spots, and blemishes on the body of Christ bring much shame and reproach to the Lord, as the world mocks the hypocrisy of their immorality when their sins are brought to light.

4) Balaam the false prophet, is self-deceived and self-deluded, as he sports himself with his own

deceiving, while feasting right in the middle of genuine Christians who walk with the Lord. The false prophets are most effective right in the middle of the Church, among Christians whom he has manipulated with many vain words, and boastings.

5) In reality they are wells without water, have gone dry, where once the Spirit of the Lord had brought refreshing water through their ministries. They are clouds of a storm, surrounding their lives is the presence of evil. However, it is the kind of evil which appears appealing and seductive. Many chase after the false prophet, as they allure through the lusts of the flesh, and many desires, those who are clean can run from the false prophets, knowing the demonic power of seduction which they possess.

6) They love the wages of unrighteousness. A covetousness heart, hard as stone, seared by the hypocrisy of immorality, in dire pursuit of exploiting the body of Christ. Balaam would sell his soul for money and sex, and pervert the Church in the process.

7) They promise you liberty, great swelling words, of great revivals and moves of God, but they themselves are slaves to corruption. For by what a man is overcome by, the same is enslaved by.

8) The have become dogs and pigs in their corruption. For after escaping the corruption in the world by a genuine faith in Christ, they go

back from the Lord, being entangled again in a life of perversion. It would have been better to not have known the way, and turn from the Lord, as a dog which returns to its own vomit, and a pig after being washed goes back to wallowing in the mud.

9) Their latter end is worse than their beginning. A great Judgement has come upon them for they have become reprobates. A gross danger of being judged by God unto the mist of darkness, which is one of the severest judgments which a fallen Christian can receive.

Is it mercy to judge a man who has exhibited the same traits of Balaam the false prophet in the New Testament Church? If we love the body of Christ, we will heed the warning of false prophets, and expose their hypocrisy to the utmost. As it is an act of mercy upon the madness of the prophet himself.

2 Peter 2:9-22
9 The Lord knoweth how to deliver the godly out of temptations, and to reserve the unjust unto the day of judgment to be punished:10 But chiefly them that walk after the flesh in the lust of uncleanness and despise government. Presumptuous are they, self-willed, they are not afraid to speak evil of dignities.

11 Whereas angels, which are greater in power and might, bring not railing accusation against them before the Lord.

12 But these, as natural brute beasts, made to be taken and destroyed, speak evil of the things that they understand not; and shall utterly perish in their own corruption.

13 And shall receive the reward of unrighteousness, as they that count it pleasure to riot in the daytime. Spots they are and blemishes, sporting themselves with their own deceivings while they feast with you.

14 Having eyes full of adultery, and that cannot cease from sin; beguiling unstable souls: an heart they have exercised with covetous practices; cursed children:

15 Which have forsaken the right way, and are gone astray, following the way of Balaam the son of Bosor, who loved the wages of unrighteousness.

16 But was rebuked for his iniquity: the dumb ass speaking with man's voice forbad the madness of the prophet.

17 These are wells without water, clouds that are carried with a tempest; to whom the mist of darkness is reserved for ever.

18 For when they speak great swelling words of vanity, they allure through the lusts of the flesh, through much wantonness, those that were clean escaped from them who live in error.

19 While they promise them liberty, they themselves are the servants of corruption: for of whom a man is overcome, of the same is he brought in bondage.

20 For if after they have escaped the pollutions of the world through the knowledge of the Lord and Saviour Jesus Christ, they are again entangled therein, and overcome, the latter end is worse with them than the beginning.

21 For it had been better for them not to have known the way of righteousness, than, after they have known it, to turn from the holy commandment delivered unto them.

22 But it is happened unto them according to the true proverb, The dog is turned to his own vomit again; and the sow that was washed to her wallowing in the mire.

Judging the Prophets

What is a true New Testament Prophet? In the Charismatic Movement this question needs great clarification and accountability. Are there any prophets today which are of the stature of an Old Testament like Elijah, Jeremiah, or John the Baptist? The answer is clearly no, as no New Testament prophet speaks the infallible word of the Lord. The message given New Testament prophets has already been given to them and are recorded in the Scriptures as the doctrines of Jesus Christ. You will see no New Testament prophets bringing in their own private interpretations of prophecy. It is forbidden as even the original 12 New Testament apostles were taught the doctrines of Jesus Christ. Apostle Paul clearly acknowledges he was taught the Gospel by Christ Himself. Also, anyone who teaches or preaches another Gospel is accursed by God. Do not let anyone go beyond what has already been established in the Scriptures. Also, do not let anyone who calls themselves an apostle or prophet say they have been given new light of revelation on old warn out interpretations of Scriptures. You are in danger of following a false prophet and heretic.

The true prophets preach the Cross, Jesus Christ, and His crucifixion. True prophets have a passion to impart the knowledge of Christ through giving the saints the meat of Gods written word. Their primary mission is to develop the saints into the fulness of the stature which belongs to Christ. True prophets come forth with sound doctrines which cause the saints to grow up into Him, which is Christ, the head of the Church, the body of Christ. That we being no longer children tossed to and fro by every wind of doctrine, and the cunningness of man. Which means the true prophets have real discernment knowing the difference between the authentic and imitation. Which leads us to one of the major issues in modern day prophets and prophetic ministry. The false prophetic cannot discern between dreams and visions which are from God, and those which come from evil spirits. Much of what is said by the prophets came from a dream, or a vision, or an angel is in fact evil spirits imitating the things of God. A New Testament Prophet must know when revelations and spiritual experiences are not from God.

The restraint a prophet must have, self-control a fruit of the Spirit is a must when being pressured to give a word of prophecy. Modern prophets are being compelled to tell everyone they are around the prophetic experiences they are having or pushed to give a word of prophecy. If you are being pushed all the time to predict or prophesy, you are being manipulated by the flesh and evil spirits. The spirit of the prophets are subject to the prophets. You are not being pushed or forced by God, or by angels, or by dreams or visions. All this open heavens anything goes has created a false prophetic ministry with angels of light, and familiar spirits of the occult which are being passed along as the Spirit of God. Let us be straight forward, anyone who says they are a prophet and teaches on portals into heaven, or astral travel in the spirit is operating in occult counterfeits. In true prophetic ministry you cannot direct or guide visions, or angels, or encounters upon demand. You are functioning in a false Holy Spirit and are being deceived by evil spirits. Only God determines who and when a true vision, dream or angelic encounter will happen. No prophet, apostle, or Christian mystic can play Holy Spirit.

This rule is steadfast and without exceptions and has become the primary reason so many false predictions and false prophetic manifests today. If you are a New Testament prophet, you are not guiding and directing the Church. Your prophetic predictions are futile as the Holy Spirit has been given to every born-again child of

God. For as many are led of the Spirit these are the Sons of God. Your Presidential predictions are cannon fodder, they mean nothing, and are only sensational. What has been the recent failures of many so-called Trump prophets? They are trying to direct the Church through false predictions which are based upon a false Gospel.

Trump Prophets believe God has exalted President Trump as a modern-day Cyrus as a savior of the nation. No man has been given that position or responsibility, as corruption deep in the government is in the hearts of those are lost in sin. Christian government is not possible in a fallen world whose Prince is the Power of the Air. Satan and the kingdom of darkness have been given authority in the nations to deceive, and government is one of their primary ways of corruption. Only the Cross of Jesus Christ can deliver men from the Kingdom of Darkness, that is why the false prophets falsely predict a Christian government will save the nation. The falsely predicted Trump would be the person to lead the Christian government into a great international revival. Every time the Trump prophets attempt to predict this manmade philosophical belief they were prophesying against the Scriptures.

To discern the prophets as false is easy as they invalidate what has already been written. They keep attempting to direct the Church into a false mission by using prophetic predictions against the authority of Scriptures. Hence the prophetic looms large as an anti-

Scriptural movement. It has become so epidemic; a false prophet was celebrated inside the Movement for rewriting the Scriptures changing thousands of Scriptural passages because of a false Jesus took him into heaven and commissioned him to do so. Today false prophets are inside the Prophetic Movement and have been exposed by all their failed and false predictions. Yet are celebrated as God's prophets.

Ephesians 4:11-16
11 And he gave some, apostles; and some, prophets; an d some, evangelists; and some, pastors andteachers;
12 For the perfecting of the saints, for the work of the ministry, for the edifying of the body of Christ:
13 Till we all come in the unity of the faith, and of the knowledge of the Son of God, unto a perfect
man, unto the measure of the stature of the fulness of Christ:
14 That we henceforth be no more children, tossed to and fro, and carried about with every wind of doctrine, by the sleight of men, and cunning craftiness, whereby they lie in wait to deceive;
15 But speaking the truth in love, may grow
up into him in all things, which is the head, even Christ:
16 From whom the whole body fitly joined
together and compacted by that
which every joint supplieth, according to the effectual working in the measure of
every part, maketh increase of the body unto the edifying of itself in love.

Marketing Dreams and Visions

Imagine living in a Church world where there is not internet, or any other form of an instant audience of hundreds or thousands of peoples. The only communication comes from your phone call, a few close friends, and Church family. Now God from time to time gives you prophetic dreams, and some are very alarming warning dreams. Since you only have a few people to share the dreams with, you bear the burden of the warning dreams in prayer. In no way are you able to create a sensational following, a platform of ministry, or any kind of popularity or financial gain. There is no push on your part to make a name for yourself, or have people identify you as a prophet. The Church is not pushing dreams and visions, so no sensationalism is present when a dream or vision comes from God. Have you ever considered this is how the Church of the first century Christians experienced the leading of the Holy Spirit?

What happens when marketing is taken out of the picture? No personal profit, no money, no fame, no glorification, or idolatry being pushed upon those who have dreams or a vision. The marketing of dreams and visions simply does not happen as there is no market for it. As the result, the Holy Spirit disperses the dreams and visions throughout the whole of the Church, and there are no exalted superstars, or self-proclaimed prophets. The central part of ministry comes from preaching and teaching the Written Word of God, and prayer, seeking knowledge and wisdom in these more foundational ways. The Church's mission is to make disciples so preaching the Gospel is always brought before the people as a main direction and focus. As making new disciples comes with a level of persecution and rejection the Church is not all caught up with mysticism and supernatural experiences. I trust this is the ordinary way God moves in His Church when the prophetic ministry is in proper order.

Now, how corrupting is the technique of marketing dreams and visions as prophetic words for the Churches consumption. The invasion of dreams and visions from all manner of peoples who are seeking an audience and want to profit from the Church. How Satan has gained a footing when the prophetic ministry can be bought and sold as a product. The purity and innocence is removed, and the restraints which prevent excess, and errors are lowered or eliminated altogether. Money, fame, prestige, and power are brought into play. It is no longer about dreams from God, visions from the Holy Spirit. Instead, it has become more about getting a word from God, so to have a platform. It is like the Church will market a man who always declaring I have a dream, God has given men a vision, or an angel came to visit me. It has become the sensation of Christians running after a man or woman who markets dreams and visions.

Let put this frankly, once you promote yourself you are doomed to marketing your ministry the rest of the time. In order to stay relevant, you must produce the next sensational dream, vision, or visitations. Your whole Christian experience will be reduced to producing revelations for Christians to consume for spiritual highs. Today, this is the state of the modern Prophetic Movement, a big marketing machine spitting out thousands of prophetic words, predictions, dreams, visions, and angelic encounters. Those who are sucked in and trapped are forced to produce or lose their audience. Without a consumer driven audience there is no money to keep the self-proclaimed prophets in business. Those who stand outside and will not enter into the deception, are constantly warning Christians of the Satanic traps.

How difficult for Christians who are seduced into following supernatural experiences, having a craving for encounters which are spiritual in nature. A consuming culture has demanded the prophets must produce, or else lose any relevance which has made them rich and famous. Sadly, Satan has gained a large footprint, and is willing to supply the Prophetic Movement with all manner of lying, dreams, and visions. Only those who hunger for righteousness will escape the great lure of modern prophetic ministry.

Jeremiah 23:14-40

[14] I have seen also in the prophets of Jerusalem an horrible thing: they commit adultery, and walk in lies: they strengthen also the hands of evildoers, that none doth return from his wickedness; they are all of them unto me as Sodom, and the inhabitants thereof as Gomorrah. [15] Therefore thus saith the LORD of hosts concerning the prophets; Behold, I will feed them with wormwood, and make them drink the water of gall: for from the prophets of Jerusalem is profaneness gone forth into all the land. [16] Thus saith the LORD of hosts, Hearken not unto the words of the prophets that prophesy unto you: they make you vain: they speak a vision of their own heart, and not out of the mouth of the LORD. [17] They say still unto them that despise me, The LORD hath said, Ye shall have peace; and they say unto every one that walketh after the imagination of his own heart, No evil shall come upon you. [18] For who hath stood in the counsel of the LORD, and hath perceived and heard his word? who hath marked his word, and heard it? [19] Behold, a whirlwind of the LORD is gone forth in fury, even a grievous whirlwind: it shall fall grievously upon the head of the wicked. [20] The anger of the LORD shall not return, until he have executed, and till he have performed the thoughts of his heart: in the latter days ye shall consider it perfectly. [21] I have not sent these prophets, yet they ran: I have not spoken to them, yet they prophesied. [22] But if they had stood in my counsel, and had caused my people to hear my words, then they should have turned them from their evil way, and from the evil of their doings. [23] Am I a God at hand,

saith the LORD, and not a God afar off?[24] Can any hide himself in secret places that I shall not see him? saith the LORD. Do not I fill heaven and earth? saith the LORD.[25] I have heard what the prophets said that prophesy lies in my name, saying, I have dreamed, I have dreamed.[26] How long shall this be in the heart of the prophets that prophesy lies? yea, they are prophets of the deceit of their own heart;[27] Which think to cause my people to forget my name by their dreams which they tell every man to his neighbour, as their fathers have forgotten my name for Baal.[28] The prophet that hath a dream, let him tell a dream; and he that hath my word, let him speak my word faithfully. What is the chaff to the wheat? saith the LORD.[29] Is not my word like as a fire? saith the LORD; and like a hammer that breaketh the rock in pieces?[30] Therefore, behold, I am against the prophets, saith the LORD, that steal my words everyone from his neighbour.[31] Behold, I am against the prophets, saith the LORD, that use their tongues, and say, He saith.[32] Behold, I am against them that prophesy false dreams, saith the LORD, and do tell them, and cause my people to err by their lies, and by their lightness; yet I sent them not, nor commanded them: therefore they shall not profit this people at all, saith the LORD.[33] And when this people, or the prophet, or a priest, shall ask thee, saying, What is the burden of the LORD? thou shalt then say unto them, What burden? I will even forsake you, saith the LORD.[34] And as for the prophet, and the priest, and the people, that shall say, The burden of the LORD, I will even punish that man and his house.[35] Thus shall ye say everyone to his neighbour, and every one to his brother, What hath the LORD answered? and, What hath the LORD spoken?[36] And the burden of the LORD shall ye mention no more: for every man's word shall be his burden; for ye have perverted the words of the living God, of the LORD of hosts our God.[37] Thus shalt thou say to the prophet, What hath the LORD answered thee? and, What hath the LORD spoken?[38] But since ye say, The burden of the LORD; therefore thus saith the LORD; Because ye say this word, The burden of the LORD, and I have sent unto you, saying, Ye shall not say, The burden of the LORD;[39] Therefore, behold, I, even I, will utterly forget you, and I will forsake you, and the city that I gave you and your fathers, and cast you out of my presence:[40] And I will bring an everlasting reproach upon you, and a perpetual shame, which shall not be forgotten.

Chapter Four
Christians As False Prophets

I Am A Prophet
I would guess thousands of Charismatic Christians identify with this statement, believing these selves to be a New Testament prophet, or prophetess. 90% of these Charismatics speak in tongues, along with 250 million Christians worldwide who proclaim the Charismatic experience. Are Evangelicals right to teach tongues and prophecy have passed away? The apostle Paul taught

on the gift of tongues, Paul said tongues is not "vain babbling," instead tongues is spoken to God in a mystery, so no man, not even the one speaking in "unknown tongues," understands what they are saying. Paul went on to say he spoke in tongues more than anyone else and instructed the Church not to stop Christians from speaking in tongues. However, everything should be done in decent order, so as not to bring confusion into the Church.

1 Corinthians 14:2

2 For he that speaketh in an unknown tongue speaketh not unto men, but unto God: for no man understandeth him; howbeit in the spirit he speaketh mysteries.

Paul also confirmed the gift of prophecy, and the reality of New Testament Prophets.

1 Corinthians 14:3

3 But he that prophesieth speaketh unto men to edification, and exhortation, and comfort.

1 Corinthians 14:29-32

29 Let the prophets speak two or three and let the other judge.

30 If anything be revealed to another that sitteth by, let the first hold his peace.

31 For ye may all prophesy one by one, that all may learn, and all may be comforted.

32 And the spirits of the prophets are subject to the prophets.

With the Scriptures teaching the proper use of the gifts of the Holy Spirit, why so many problems with Charismatics in the gift of prophecy, and so many Charismatics declaring they are prophets? The first thing is simple, if you give false prophecies, consistently over and over, how does this make you a prophet by any definition? False and failed predictive words have dominated the Charismatic prophetic by the thousands and are basically overlooked and excused. Is this the way Paul taught New Testament prophecy to function? A man or woman who declares they are a prophet who consistently gives false predictive words of prophecy, cannot be a "true prophet" no matter how popular. Your false prophecy proves you follow the wrong spirit, a spirit of error, and you are a danger to the body of Christ.

What happens when a prophet or prophetess teach or preach false doctrines? Can they be a "messenger for Jesus Christ?" How can a person who teaches doctrines against the Written Word of God, be God's prophet? So many who are declared to be prophets cannot even properly teach Bible doctrine. How does the preaching of false doctrines, heresy, and doctrines of demons make for a New Testament prophet? At best you are a false prophet, living in the flesh, even though you are a brother in Christ. At worse false prophets are "wolves in sheep's clothing," and are destroyers of God's flock. If you are a man or woman who is being exposed for teaching false doctrine, and you think you are a prophet get out of the ministry, until a proper foundation of the doctrines of Christ has been developed in your life. Leading the Church into deception draws the curse of God, you are accursed, and under God's judgment.

Here is another issue. Prophecy is not about proclaiming your favorite doctrine, and then putting a "thus says the Lord," label on it. False doctrine, given as prophecy is an abomination. It is the worse of the worse in the false and lying prophetic. So many high-profile prophets in the Charismatic Movement have perverted the doctrines of Christ, by making prophetic words a doctrinal statement. The Holy Spirit will not prophesy against the written Word of God, as the Spirit and Word agree. When a Charismatic prophet attempts to predict another worldwide revival, and Church take overusing prophecy as the vehicle, this is a corrupt and dangerous practice. Charismatic style prophets have generated a whole system of false prophecy which promotes doctrines of demons as the word of the Lord.

So, what happens when instead of preaching or teaching your favorite doctrine of demons, or heresy, you prophesy it as a Word of God instead? You are seducing and controlling the Church, using the ignorance of Christians who lack knowledge and discernment. You have become a grave danger to the Church, function in a spirit of error, and have fallen to Satan's trap. You are a heretic, a false teacher, who is to be "marked by the Church," warned about, and rejected after you have been confronted two or three times. In essence you are a false prophet spreading your cancerous leaven throughout the Church. The fact that you are uncorrectable demonstrations you understand little of the true accountability. Which the New Testament demands of words of prophecy, and New Testament prophets which must have their words continuously judged, by what has already been written.

A Prophet who hides behind popularity, who is continuously exposed for false predictive prophecy, and teaching of doctrines of demons, has become normalized inside the Prophetic Charismatic Movement. This can never be the work of the Holy Spirit instead the work of the Antichrist spirit.

1 John 4:1-6
1 Beloved, believe not every spirit, but try the spirits whether they are of God: because many false prophets are gone out into the world.
2 Hereby know ye the Spirit of God: Every spirit that confesseth that Jesus Christ is come in the flesh is of God:
3 And every spirit that confesseth not that Jesus Christ is come in the flesh is not of God: and this is that spirit of antichrist, whereof ye have heard that it should come; and even now already is it in the world.

4 Ye are of God, little children, and have overcome them: because greater is he that is in you, than he that is in the world.

5 They are of the world: therefore, speak they of the world, and the world heareth them.

6 We are of God: he that knoweth God heareth us; he that is not of God heareth not us. Hereby know we the spirit of truth, and the spirit of error.

The Lords Prophets

The standards of prophetic ministry have been severally compromised by the Charismatic Movement. For years false prophetic predictions have been marketed as prophetic words from the Lord. Now with the failed Trump prophecies the Prophetic Movement is scrambling to stop the criticism which has come from inside and outside the organized Church. I trust the Charismatic prophets would just like to get on with it and begin their litany of prophecies once again. It is ironic many self-declared prophets who falsely predicted the Trump reelection, are now attempting to correct the excess and errors. The problem many of these prophets are not wanting to lose their fan base but were also the greatest offenders leading thousands of Charismatics astray. It is a bit hypocritical after years of book writing, conferences, and heavy presence from social media now to act like they can remove the sliver of the false prophetic, when they have had logs in their own eyes. Wanting to maintain the status of being a prophet but lacking in the real fruits as written in Scriptures.

So, what are some characteristics Christians should look for when judging the Lord's prophets? Here are some things to consider:

1) A prophet from the Old Testament or the New Testament should have prophetic accuracy. If the prophet of the Lord speaks by inspiration of the Holy Spirit, then prophet words are truthful, accurate, and come to pass. Why would the prophetic Movement in any measure justify false prophecy and failed predictions? The fruit of true prophets is speaking true prophetic words. It is just that simple. Once that standard is removed all manner of demonic lies and deception will be passed off as prophetic words. When Charismatics abandon true prophetic words, and accept the counterfeit and sensational, then false prophets will abound.

2) A true prophet must be called by God, and not by man. Many are the self-appointed men and women who say they are the Lord's prophet. How destructive to put yourself into a ministry God has never called you for or appointed you to do. Thousands of Charismatics believe

themselves to be prophets in the Movement, being filled with all manner of vain imaginations. It is hard to believe the "strange personalities and put-on personas" which are put off as prophetic personalities. How strange to watch the parade of weirdness, and gimmicks which are a performance from actors, playing like they are prophets. It is like if you do not have some gimmick, you cannot attract enough audience. The pretense play acting is what has been passed off as the prophetic.

3) Prophets called by the Lord are fewer in number than the thousands of the self-proclaimed. When false prophetic ministry is marketed by the Movement as true prophets, then authentic prophets will not be allowed place. The Charismatic Movement needs to consider false prophets never called or chosen by the Lord may outnumber true prophets 1000 to 1. Why would the Lord choose a man or woman who lacks the character to restrain himself from always attracting an audience by marketing supposed dreams, visions, or angelic visitations. The apostle Paul was also a prophet of the Lord with an abundance of prophet experiences, but you do not see the exploitation of the Church by Paul marketing an abundance of revelations.

4) Why would the Lord call a man who will never
    have the character or the integrity to stand in
    the prophets' ministry? The lack of character in
    those who say are prophets, has been
    continuously overlooked by leaders across the
    board. When a man or woman speaks false
    prophecy, character issues need to be seriously
    examined. Should the Lord's prophet be led by
    lies, deception, spiritual blindness, a lack of
    discernment. Aren't prophets to be known for
    the keen discernment, knowing the authentic
    from the imitation? It takes a lot of humility to
    be restrained by the Lord, not to misrepresent
    the testimony of the Lord. Simply put, many self-
    proclaimed prophets need to be "seen all the
    time." More often than not the Lord's prophet is
    hidden, walking with the Lord in submission, not
    seeking self-promotion or vain glory. How can
    the Lord's prophet speak for the Lord when
    seeking glory from man?

4) The passion of the Lord's prophets is to call
    God's people into a deep surrender. The call to
    repentance is a hallmark of true prophets of the
    Lord. Prophets will preach or teach with a
    prophetic ability, which has an inspirational
    component. You will often "hear the voice of

prophecy in their preaching and teaching." Mature prophets can speak with deep conviction coming from a life or personal brokenness. In fact, one of the ear marks of genuine prophets is a life marked with suffering. A truly broken vessel through whom the Holy Spirit can cry out with the prophetic voice, "prepare the way of the Lord." A proud man is diametrically opposed to the true character of the Lord's prophets. Of course, an immoral man, is just a wolf in sheep's clothing. A multimillionaire prophet is a contradiction, as false prophets are lovers of money.

1 John 4:1-5

4 Beloved, believe not every spirit, but try the spirits whether they are of God: because many false prophets are gone out into the world.
[2] Hereby know ye the Spirit of God: Every spirit that confesseth that Jesus Christ is come in the flesh is of God:
[3] And every spirit that confesseth not that Jesus Christ is come in the flesh is not of God: and this is that spirit of antichrist, whereof ye have heard that it should come; and even now already is it in the world.
[4] Ye are of God, little children, and have overcome them: because greater is he that is in you, than he that is in the world.

[5] They are of the world: therefore, speak they of the world, and the world heareth them.
[6] We are of God: he that knoweth God heareth us; he that is not of God heareth not us. Hereby know we the spirit of truth, and the spirit of error.

The Temptation To Be Great

Perhaps the Church has not understood the influence of the world, its worldly success and image. One of the world's great temptations is often celebrated by the Church, the desire to be great. Almost no one would argue about being great in the eyes of other people. However, in the economy of God, the principles of the Christian faith are often the complete opposite from the world's values. For example, in God's eyes those who serve others, preferring others needs before their own making themselves the least is great in God, and are great in the Kingdom of Heaven. Looking like a great man in the eyes of the world is often accompanied with pride and self-exaltation. You cannot be great in God by exalting yourself, and using people to get what you want, fame, power, money, all the treasures of the world.

In modern organized Christianity you will often see the exaltation of men by members of the body of Christ putting man into a position God has never intended. Those who rule over other men, exploit the Church making millions of dollars by using ministry to build a religious kingdom with followers. Jesus Christ warned His disciples of seeking the praise and fame of men. All the works are to be seen of men, love the upper rooms and chief seats. Call no man your father on earth, for one is your Father in heaven. This is in direct reference to religious rulers and leaders. The Pope is not your father, your favorite Charismatic apostles are not your spiritual fathers. These are written in Scriptures as there is only one exalted head over the Church, Jesus Christ who is our High Priest, and Jesus Christ is the apostle of our profession of faith. The rest of the Church are just servants even if they hold titles like apostle, prophet, pastor or elder. Nether be called masters, for one is your master even Christ.

What you see in modern day ministry with high visibility is entitlement. When men have exalted men into ungodly idolatry, religious pride, we see men use their fame, exaltation, and pride to promote the building of their agendas. It takes a lot of money to stay at the top, a great deal of getting your name out, holding onto the platforms of fame. In this position we have seen the Church overlook sin, human weakness, works of the flesh, because we need to keep our idols "propped up" lest the fall down and are exposed for the frail men which they really are.

God is not looking for great men, great leaders, eloquent speakers, neither is He looking for a Church of

Great world conquers. These are all the standards of pride, the strength of man-made glory. God is looking for men and women who are of a broken and contrite spirit. Blessed are the meek, who do not strive to build kingdoms after their image, for the meek are the true inheritors of the coming Kingdom age. The meek are broken submitted, and dependent upon the Lord. The meek shall inherit the earth.

Blessed are the poor in spirit for theirs is the kingdom of heaven. Will the mighty men who strive with pride and ambition to be great be the inheritors of the Kingdom of heaven? Their kingdom is now built upon the ambition and glory of man, they are the men whose praise is sung among men. However, men of greatness and glory are not those who suffer reproach for the sake of Jesus Christ. Beware when men speak well of you, and you are rich and famous as the result of their praise.

For you have your reward now, the praise of men and the worlds riches. The meek, those who suffer as servants of the Lord, those who do not layup treasures on earth, using the Church to build kingdoms of self-glory who suffer with the Lord making themselves of no reputation, great is your future reward. For so suffered Jesus Christ making Himself the servant of all. For those who will be great in the Kingdom of Heaven will be made low as servants of the Lord. For whoever would be great in the Lord let him be the servant of all.

Matthew 5:11-12

11 Blessed are ye, when men shall revile you, and persecute you, and shall say all manner of evil against you falsely, for my sake.

12 Rejoice and be exceeding glad: for great is your reward in heaven: for so persecuted they the prophets which were before you.

Matthew 23:5-12

5 But all their works they do for to be seen of men: they make broad their phylacteries, and enlarge the borders of their garments,

6 And love the uppermost rooms at feasts, and the chief seats in the synagogues,

7 And greetings in the markets, and to be called of men, Rabbi, Rabbi.

8 But be not ye called Rabbi: for one is your Master, even Christ; and all ye are brethren.

9 And call no man your father upon the earth: for one is your Father, which is in heaven.

10 Neither be ye called masters: for one is your Master, even Christ.

11 But he that is greatest among you shall be your servant.

12 And whosoever shall exalt himself shall be abased; and he that shall humble himself shall be exalted.

Matthew 20:21-28

21 And he said unto her, What wilt thou? She saith unto him, Grant that these my two sons may sit, the one on

thy right hand, and the other on the left, in thy kingdom.

22 But Jesus answered and said, Ye know not what ye ask. Are ye able to drink of the cup that I shall drink of, and to be baptized with the baptism that I am baptized with? They say unto him, We are able.

23 And he saith unto them, Ye shall drink indeed of my cup, and be baptized with the baptism that I am baptized with: but to sit on my right hand, and on my left, is not mine to give, but it shall be given to them for whom it is prepared of my Father.

24 And when the ten heard it, they were moved with indignation against the two brethren.

25 But Jesus called them unto him, and said, Ye know that the princes of the Gentiles exercise dominion over them, and they that are great exercise authority upon them.

26 But it shall not be so among you: but whosoever will be great among you, let him be your minister.

27 And whosoever will be chief among you, let him be your servant:

28 Even as the Son of man came not to be ministered unto, but to minister, and to give his life a ransom for many.

Chapter Five
Prophets Old and New

Let us get real the Bible teaches a lot about Prophets, both Old Testament and New Testament. The warnings given in the New Testament concerning false prophets is vast, by Jesus Christ and many of the original apostles. Why would there be warnings about false prophets in the Church if no real New Testament Prophets even existed. It would be silly to warn about false prophets if no authentic prophets exists, as every man or woman who declared themselves a prophet would be false. Sadly, today that is more of the reality, many who proclaim they are an apostle, or a prophet simply are not. The worse of the worse, is the high visibility ones are often false prophets, with false predictive prophetic words. The number of false prophecies in the Prophetic Movement is staggering, making the prophetic a perversion of the real. Simply put when the Prophetic Movement celebrates a man to rewrite hundreds of Scriptures, adding words or subtracting them to change their original meanings, just because he says Jesus appeared to him in a vision, and took him to heaven, then you know the whole Movement has fallen to demonic counterfeits.

So how could you expect a modern-day New Testament prophet to function or be fruitful in the modern organized Charismatic Church? Let us be clear, no modern prophet, gets "new light," on the Scriptures to rewrite Scriptures. The Bible is a set book with "infallible doctrine and prophecies," none of what the Holy Spirit has inspired men who wrote the Scriptures will fail in the smallest measure. Any man or woman who presumes on Scriptures to "add new light," is a false prophet, no matter how popular their name of their ministry. There is an extraordinary number of false apostles and prophets inside the Prophetic Charismatic Movement who " add their philosophy" or personal opinions to Scriptures. Who undermine the infallibility , the immutably of God' s Written Word? In this way it is easy to identify false prophets because the preach and teach false doctrines, and heresies. When confronted with the authority of Scriptures as to their false teachings, they refuse correction, falsely assuming their perversion of Scriptures is "accurate teaching." In effect they will not repent and will not stop teaching their doctrines of demons.

The main function of a New Testament prophet is to teach and preach the doctrines of Scriptures, without any perversion, twisting of Scriptures, doctrines of demons, or heresies. The best of New Testament prophets are powerful preachers of the word, who can preach inspirationally, bringing great exhortation from the Word of God. A good example of a New Testament prophet would be David Wilkerson. David would call the Church to repentance, confront sin, preach the Cross, and warn of the coming judgment and wrath of God. David Wilkerson would preach Jesus Christ and Him crucified and give clear warning to escape the wrath of God. David Wilkerson would also receive revelatory experiences a dream or a vision, which confirmed the Scriptures, and brought "heightened awareness," to the doctrine which had already been written. Keith Green is another example of a modern-day prophet, where God used Keith's music to speak and preach the Gospel.

The first responsibility of a modern-day prophet is to preach and teach the Gospel of Jesus Christ. Just look at the apostle Paul, who came out from among the prophets and teachers of Antioch. Paul wrote his message was Jesus Christ and Him crucified, and he would not glory in anything else except the Cross. Now if the man God used to write the majority of the New Testament said the message of the Church is not signs and wonders, Instead is the preaching of the Cross who are modern day prophets to say otherwise. Who, are modern day apostles and prophets to exalt themselves over the written Word of God? Let' get this clear, no modern apostle will ever carry the weight of an apostle Paul, or one of the original twelve apostles. That also goes for any modern-day prophets, will never even match the infallibility of what was spoken by Old Testament Prophets. If your think the standard for New Testament Prophets is the same or greater than the Old Testament prophets, then the majority of your prophetic voices would be dead in Old Testament days. Being stoned to death for giving false prophecies, and as a false prophet.

What is the problem today with those who identify as prophets? They will not preach or teach the doctrines of Christ, and they have put the gift of prophecy before the Written Word of God. They have twisted and perverted the gift of prophecy, until they function more like New Age prophets with fortune telling and psychic abilities. Just let me be blunt, not everything which comes supernaturally by revelation is coming from the Holy Spirit. Just because they can get your name, address, and birth dates, does not mean they speak for God. When a man begins to give personal information, and then says I have a vision of one of your dead relatives in heaven, and begins to pass information from the dead to the living, how is this not "necromancy," and the person "not a Christian psychic?"

Let us get real the New Testament prophet was never about fortune telling like we see in the Charismatic Movement today. What is being pawned off as prophetic words is often nothing more than soul power and psychic ability. Many who proclaim trips into heaven upon demand are simply practicing astral travel, leaving their bodies, and dealing with angels of light who seduce them to believe there are encountering heaven and God.

Why would New Age Witchcraft not invade the Prophetic Movement as they teach it has been stolen from the Church as must be recovered. Today the New Age is being practiced, fortune telling, psychic predictions, tarot cards, astral travel, mind power, it is a complete perversion not coming from the Holy Spirit, the Testimony of Jesus which is the true Spirit of prophecy. New Age prophets abound today, and they are some of Charismatics favorite mystic apostles and prophets. Their magic show must go on and the body of Christ is willing to pay them millions to teach their magical craft.

The Prophets Burden

The Scriptures inform us of prophets of the Lord found both in Old Testament and New Testament passages. It is enough the Bible recognizes the prophets of the Lord, even when the people do not, which is true to this very day. What is the problem, the false prophets outnumber the true prophets 1000 to one? So, many in the Church have come to despise the prophetic ministry, or completely the opposite entertains the false prophets. Either way, the true prophets are not easily heard, or often not received by the mainstream of Gods people. This picture is historically true both in the Old Testament and the New Testament. A prophet is not without honor except in his own country and with his own family. Basically, the true prophet of the Lord is sent to call Gods wayward people back to the Lord.

The calling of a prophet includes the Lord's burden. A yoke set upon the prophet by the Lord, a difficult word, a correction a rebuke. Warning Gods people to set your house in order and prepare to meet the Lord. John the Baptist is a good example of calling Israel into repentance to prepare for their Messiah, whom the nation by in large would reject. John himself, though revered as a prophet would be beheaded by confronting the sexual perversity of the King.

What is the burden of the Lord today? The sun is setting on both the world and the Church. Twilight is come, the time just before the long dark night. The Church is very noisy with manmade philosophies, God is trying to silence the Church, but men get offended when you shut their tongues from all their clamoring. Twilight is a dangerous time, just a little light remains, it signals a time when subtly is about to fill the earth. The time right before the Great Tribulation, the blackness of the night. The children of the night will reveal in the darkness, for they do not know the flood is about to come and take them all away. The prophets of the Lord are warning of an apostasy, a falling away, for it is in the time of twilight the subtle woman comes, the adulteress to seduce the Church with her smooth words and speech.

The burden of the Lord is to warn the people the world is growing dark, the Church must prepare for the midnight hour, watch, and pray, lest being overtaken by the snare which is coming upon the whole world. Do not many just think it is already determined, they will be taken from the dark days, and yet the Lord said watch and pray, so you would not be overtaken. The Church is making light of the evil day, right before their eyes, adulterers and adulteress who live immoral lives find a home in the Church. Worship the Lord and say with impudent hearts I have done no wrong. The false Shepard's sooths their conscience with false messages of love, a siren song, and will not confront their wickedness.

It is twilight, the adulteress Church is on the rise, for the say the Lord is a far off and will not return for some while. Let us love like the world, as the Lord loves us in our sins. The burden of the Lord. "You adulterers and adulteress do you not know friendship with the world, makes you an enmity with God. Therefore, whoever will be a friend with the world is the enemy of God." Sinning saint of God are you now become Gods enemy and do not even know it. For the false prophets speak to you a false message saying peace, peace when there is no peace.

The prophet's burden remains the same, "repent and make ready for the coming of the Lord." For the Pharisaical Adulteress Church, "who has warned you to flee from the coming wrath of God?"

Proverbs 7:5-27
5 That they may keep thee from the strange woman, from the stranger which flattereth with her words.
6 For at the window of my house I looked through my casement,
7 And beheld among the simple ones, I discerned among the youths, a young man void of understanding,

8 Passing through the street near her corner; and he went the way to her house,

9 In the twilight, in the evening, in the black and dark night:

10 And, behold, there met him a woman with the attire of a harlot, and subtil of heart

11 (She is loud and stubborn; her feet abide not in her house:

12 Now is she without, now in the streets, and lieth in wait at every corner.)

13 So she caught him, and kissed him, and with an impudent face said unto him,

14 I have peace offerings with me; this day have I payed my vows.

15 Therefore came I forth to meet thee, diligently to seek thy face, and I have found thee.

16 I have decked my bed with coverings of tapestry, with carved works, with fine linen of Egypt.

17 I have perfumed my bed with myrrh, aloes, and cinnamon.

18 Come, let us take our fill of love until the morning: let us solace ourselves with loves.

19 For the goodman is not at home, he is gone a long journey:

20 He hath taken a bag of money with him and will come home at the day appointed.

21 With her much fair speech she caused him to yield, with the flattering of her lips she forced him.

22 He goeth after her straightway, as an ox goeth to the slaughter, or as a fool to the correction of the stocks.

23 Till a dart strike through his liver; as a bird hasteth to the snare, and knoweth not that it is for his life.

24 Hearken unto me now therefore, O ye children, and attend to the words of my mouth.

25 Let not thine heart decline to her ways, go not astray in her paths.

26 For she hath cast down many wounded: yea, many strong men have been slain by her.

27 Her house is the way to hell, going down to the chambers of death.

Jeremiah 23:25-40

25 I have heard what the prophets said that prophesy lies in my name, saying, I have dreamed, I have dreamed.

26 How long shall this be in the heart of the prophets that prophesy lies? yea, they are prophets of the deceit of their own heart.

27 Which think to cause my people to forget my name by their dreams which they tell every man to his neighbour, as their fathers have forgotten my name for Baal.

28 The prophet that hath a dream, let him tell a dream; and he that hath my word, let him speak my word faithfully. What is the chaff to the wheat? saith the Lord.

29 Is not my word like as a fire? saith the Lord; and like a hammer that breaketh the rock in pieces?

30 Therefore, behold, I am against the prophets, saith the Lord, that steal my words everyone from his neighbour.

31 Behold, I am against the prophets, saith the Lord, that use their tongues, and say, He saith.

32 Behold, I am against them that prophesy false dreams, saith the Lord, and do tell them, and cause my people to err by their lies, and by their lightness; yet I sent them not, nor commanded them: therefore they shall not profit this people at all, saith the Lord.

33 And when this people, or the prophet, or a priest, shall ask thee, saying, What is the burden of the Lord? thou shalt then say unto them, What burden? I will even forsake you, saith the Lord.

34 And as for the prophet, and the priest, and the people, that shall say, The burden of the Lord, I will even punish that man and his house.

35 Thus shall ye say every one to his neighbour, and every one to his brother, What hath the Lord answered? and, What hath the Lord spoken?

36 And the burden of the Lord shall ye mention no more: for every man's word shall be his burden; for ye have perverted the words of the living God, of the Lord of hosts our God.

37 Thus shalt thou say to the prophet, What hath the Lord answered thee? and, What hath the Lord spoken?

38 But since ye say, The burden of the Lord; therefore thus saith the Lord; Because ye say this word, The burden of the Lord, and I have sent unto you, saying, Ye shall not say, The burden of the Lord;

39 Therefore, behold, I, even I, will utterly forget you, and I will forsake you, and the city that I gave you and your fathers, and cast you out of my presence:
40 And I will bring an everlasting reproach upon you, and a perpetual shame, which shall not be forgotten.

Is Prophecy Fortune Telling

In the Prophetic Movement prophecy has become about destiny reading, telling an unsaved person about how God sees them even when they are lost in sin. Sort of a future version of what they could be a predictive word of destiny. Is this how the gift of prophecy is supposed to function? I will just say, telling an unsaved person about their "future self," is more like fortune telling of the New Age or the occult, than the Holy Spirit gift of prophecy. Why are Christians being taught to prophesy future identity over unsaved persons as a function of the gift of prophecy? The truth is the confidence in the message of the Cross, has been undermined in the belief of bringing heavenly encounters to the lost. Instead of sharing the gospel message and leading the unsaved to faith in Jesus Christ, the emphasis is in the supernatural display of signs and wonders, and predictive words which will then save the person.

Here is another way prophecy has become more like the New Age gift of fortune telling. Should prophetic people seek to always get personal information in a supernatural way? Should Charismatics seek to get; names, addresses, birth dates, names of relatives, names of dead relatives, or see the dead in heaven and pass on comforting messages to the living from the dead? All this is being practiced and taught as "advanced prophetic gifting," or hearing from God, but is it? My answer is simple, in New Age witchcraft, psychics are taught to hear from "familiar spirits," they get personal information, and pass messages from dead friends or relatives to the living. So why should the Holy Spirit expend so much time and effort in something which is practiced by the New Age, or by psychics? Instead, the Gospel is to be preached to lead fallen men into saving faith in Christ? Do I trust Charismatics will discern familiar spirits, which will function wherever and whenever the people are open to the conditions which allow for them to do so? No, I do not trust the whole sale production of prophecy under the banner of getting personal information or seeing and speaking to the dead (Necromancy).

Why are Charismatic Christians passing New Age practices off as the work of the Holy Spirit? Simple truth is the preaching of the Cross and the teaching of the doctrines of Jesus Christ, are no longer observed. Instead, a sensuous experience with personal encounters and subjective experience has been promoted. Charismatics have become indifferent to the Word of God, and want to "feel or experience God," and plenty of Charismatic leaders have fallen into performing New Age psychic signs and wonders. Prophecy upon demand has become dangerous, as familiar spirits have worked their way into the Prophets, who want to get personal information. Can God give a name, yes, can He give a birth date or address, yes? Does God do this upon demand, absolutely not. Does God want to teach the body of Christ how to hear from God and get all this personal information? No, it opens the door to familiar spirit deception.

Ironically, true prophesy has been losing ground in the Prophetic Movement. Instead, false prophecy, false predictive words, "reading a person's desires," and fortune telling by familiar spirits have grown exponentially. All this is done under the banner of schools of the supernatural and the Extreme Prophetic. All manner of sensuous lying psychic phenomena, visions upon demand, traveling into heaven (astral projection) spirit travel, spiritual portals, talking with the dead in heaven, and angelic encounters are now taught in prophetic schools of the supernatural.

In fact, in the Charismatic prophetic many famous voices say it is proper to recover from the New Age Movement what has been stolen from the Church. Let us just say as the Prophetic Movement increases it looks more and more like the New Age Movement than prophetic, Holy Spirit filled Christianity. Can Christians develop their psychic abilities the way mediums of the New Age do? Absolutely, Satan is counting on it, and is busy inside the Prophetic Movement subverting the authentic prophetic with New Age counterfeits. For the testimony of Jesus is the Spirit of prophecy, not the sensationalism of New Age familiar spirits.

Syncretism New Age and Christianity

"One of the most persistent themes in early Christian accounts of heresy is that it smuggles rival accounts of reality into the household of faith. It is a Trojan horse, a means of establishing (whether by accident or design) an alternative belief system within its host. Heresy appears to be Christian, yet it is actually an enemy of the faith that sows the seed of faith's destruction.* It could be compared to a virus, which establishes its presence within the host, ultimately using its host's replication system to achieve dominance. Yet whatever the ultimate origins of heresy might be, the threat comes from within the community of faith."
– Alister McGrath[188]
[188]McGrath, Alister. Heresy: A History of Defending the Truth. © 2009, Harper One, Harper The Collins Publishers, New York, NY; p 34

What Is Syncretism
Syncretism /ˈsɪŋkrətɪzəm/ is the combining of different beliefs, while blending practices of various schools of thought. Syncretism involves the merging or assimilation of several originally discrete traditions, especially in the theology and mythology of religion, thus asserting an underlying unity and allowing for an inclusive approach to other faiths. Syncretism also

occurs commonly in expressions of arts and culture (known as eclecticism) as well as politics (syncretic politics).

Syncretism (/ˈsɪŋkrətɪzəm/) is the combining of different beliefs, while blending practices of various schools of thought. Syncretism involves the merging or assimilation of several originally discrete traditions, especially in the theology and mythology of religion, thus asserting an underlying unity and allowing for an inclusive approach to other faiths. (Wikipedia)

Coming Divine Man
Have you ever noticed how many times a message comes which speaks of an evolving superior man? Two major themes speak of an evolving divine man which can establish a utopian world. Of course, Charles Darwin sold the world on an ever-increasing man in Darwin's Theory of Evolution. At the same time the philosopher Hegel spoke of man's ability to establish a utopian world. We know this temptation is very real for the whole world fought WWII over this belief. An antichrist type rose to power in Germany taking Darwin's Evolution to the German nation declaring a superior race will rule the world and usher in a German utopian world. Adolf Hitler took the Aryan belief of a superior race, a superior man who would rule over the nation's first by military might. Of the Aryan Supremacy came

the murder of six million Jews who were deemed by the Germans as less than human.

Do not think the Church escapes this kind of deception, as the Church in Germany supported the rise of Hitler and Aryan supremacy. What is behind the belief of an ever-evolving better man, a conqueror to rise to power and establish a utopian world. Does not this very belief go right back to the tower of Babel and the rise of Nimrod, an antichrist type? The need for supermen to rise which are superior to other men is the basis for world rulers and tyrants, and the world history of war. Even Church history has shed blood in the name of Holy Wars, and Inquisitions when a superiority mindset of ruling the world by the Holy Catholic Empire was promoted. Ironically, the influence of Babylon still remains and will be finalized in the corrupted Church which joins herself with the Antichrist. The Great Harlot Church called Mystery Babylon the Mother of Harlots.

Why does the Charismatic Movement always speak of a coming superior race of Christians? For example, a recent emphasis has come from high visibility Charismatics who teach the coming of a "new breed," a superior type of Christian who can transform the Church and world. This super race of Christians are supposed to arise and usher in a new era. In the Charismatic Movement you will hear of super Christians with special powers and ability above and beyond what normal Church history has produced. Names of this super race of Christians are, the Elijah Company, Joel's Army, the Joseph Company, the Manifested Sons of God, and other designations which are titles of Christian conquerors.

The false doctrine of Manifested Sons of God which looks for superior race of Christians, and the conquest of the world by these supermen has plagued the Charismatic Movement for decades. Even right now you will hear of a political and militant version of a new breed of Christians to rise to power to make war with the corruption in government. Even the emphasis of Christians taking up arms and to form Christian militias to fight in a new civil war. These New Breed super Christians will arise to influence every sphere of culture, until America is restored to a Republic once again. The basis of saving America comes from God raising up the "new breed," a Manifested Son of God who is an overcomer to save America and eventually the world. Do not think Charismatics wont whole heartedly promote the supermen the super race who arise to bring divine government to the earth. Get ready for the deluge of supposed "prophetic words and predictions" which foretell of the rising of this Super Church. In reality, just like the deception in Germany which prepared the way of Adolf Hitlers rise to power, so now in the modern Charismatic Movement you can hear a similar sound of a coming super race of men. A sound which does not announce the coming of Jesus Christ, instead makes ready for the Church and world to accept the worlds next Superman, the false Messiah, the Antichrist.

Chapter Six
What Is A Prophetic Word

What Is the Holy Spirit Gift of Prophecy

Here is the New Testament definition for the gift of prophecy:
1 Corinthians 14:3
3 But he that prophesieth speaketh unto men to edification, and exhortation, and comfort.

The Word of God is not up to debate, so this not a statement on its cessation or continuation. It is a single sentence which defines the gift of prophecy as it existed in the first century Church. You cannot deny its existence back then, only the apostle Paul was teaching the Church about its function. Here are the facts 1) Prophecy is not preaching or teaching of the Scriptures. 2) Prophecy is not a special discernment given to rightly divide the written Word of God. 3) Prophecy is one of the gifts of the Holy Spirit which speaks to men in a known language. If you are English speaking a word of prophecy will be given in the English language. The simple gift of prophecy has "no supernatural revelation," like a future prediction, or revelation of present-day facts. 4) The simple gift of prophecy only has 3 elements when spoken by inspiration of the Holy

Spirit. 5) The 3 elements are edification, exhortation, and comfort. Only those elements spoken in a prophetic word is recognized as the simple gift of prophecy.

The apostle Paul also states the purpose of the Holy Spirit gift of prophecy.
1 Corinthians 14:4
4 He that speaketh in an unknown tongue edifieth himself; but he that prophesieth edifieth the church.

The original intent of the gift of prophecy was to edify the Church by a spoken word which came from the inspiration of the Holy Spirit. Prophecy in its simplest form was not preaching, or predicting the future, or visions of heaven, or angelic visitations. Instead, born-again Christians speaking a simple word of encouragement inspired by the Holy Spirit. This gift existed in the first century Church and the apostle Paul encouraged the whole Church to desire the gift of prophecy. Never did Paul put prophecy on equal authority as the Written Word of God, neither did Paul say we were to despise Prophecy.

1 Corinthians 14:39-40
39 Wherefore, brethren, covet to prophesy, and forbid not to speak with tongues.
40 Let all things be done decently and in order.

Now does the gift of prophecy exist today in modern Charismatics. Let us start with a statement many are the thousands who are saying they have a prophetic word from God. Is it the simple gift of prophecy as stated by Paul in teaching the Church at Corinth? I would say 95 % of prophetic words are about the future, or dreams, or visions, or visitations which are not the simple gift of prophecy. All most gone from existence is "the Holy Spirit inspired simple gift of prophecy given as the Lord wills." Today the Charismatic Church is overrun by mystical experiences which is labeled as the Prophetic or the Extreme Prophetic. Also has pushed the Biblical definition of prophecy out from its Biblical restraints into the New Age and occult. Simply put you will not garner large audiences or big money, and labels of being characterized as a prophet, by encouraging the Church with the simple gift of prophecy.

What is the problem, most of those who are called modern day prophets are not truly prophesying by the Holy Spirit gift of prophecy as defined by the first century Church? Since the modern gift of New Testament of prophesy does not center in anyone man, no man can become the center of attention with all men attempting to "follow the prophet." The true gift would be distributed throughout the whole body of Christ, so no man could claim a corner on prophetic words. Instead, the Holy Spirit would lead the inspiration choosing the member of the body who would be inspired to prophecy in anyone meeting to encourage, exhort, and strengthen the saints present. In the Charismatic Movement of the 1980's this is how the simple gift of prophecy functioned.

The change began when the boundaries which defined the gift of prophecy were violated by what is called the Extreme Prophetic. Today the Charismatic Church stands idly by, and watches "prophetic superstars who have the word of the Lord for them." Basically, fortune telling has subverted the leading of the Holy Spirit giving a platform for thousands of false prophetic words. So, am I supposed to submit to an inerrant false prophetic ministry which has fallen to New Age and occult practices? In no way should any Christian submit to false prophets or false prophetic words. Even in the name of Christian unity. When Charismatics attempt to justify the false prophetic ministry of today as Biblically accurate it shows how deep the deception really runs. Christians who challenge the gift of prophecy is not in existence today according to Bible standards is basically incorrect. The reason is not the gift of prophecy has passed away after the first century Church. Instead, it has been so perverted by the Charismatic Movement as to become a danger to the authentic Christian faith.

Today Charismatics have their flesh pumped up by words of prophecy which are vain glory and itch their ears according to their ungodly lusts and desires.

Are You Tired of Being Hyped With Hidden Mysteries

What is unique to the Christian faith, the hidden mystery of God has been unveiled in the person of Jesus Christ. Do you want to know the wisdom, the knowledge, the understanding which has been hidden from other ages, but know has been revealed in Christ Jesus? Let me put this simply, the mystery of God is acknowledged or known by the saints, in Christ Jesus. God and his hidden mystery is no longer a mystery, as Jesus Christ has revealed them to the saints. The wisdom and knowledge of God is summoned up in Jesus Christ in whom are all the treasures of wisdom and knowledge.

I say this lest any man should beguile you with enticing words. Are you a prophet, do you beguile the Church with the "hidden mysteries of God?" Is your message always about a hidden mystery, the unknown, the unseen, which is now revealed in your newest book? Let us get this right, prophets who depend on "esoteric hidden knowledge," by which they have access and privilege with God are marketing the Church with seduction. Esoteric hidden knowledge is the way of the Gnostic false prophets of the first century, a beguilement of the plain simple truth of Jesus Christ, twisting it into a hidden mystery. The Gnostics are the Christian Gurus, who feed off fascinating Christians with of hidden knowledge, which requires the prophets to reveal. Of course, this comes with a price monetary gain for the prophetic Guru, and the surrender of the novices will to be controlled and manipulated.

The modern prophets of the Charismatic Movement are fallen into this deception. It is always the next big revelation, a visit to heaven, a communication with angels, and speaking to dead prophets. Why all this commotion, why all this hype, to say "you have been given the keys to hidden mysteries." You are a prophetic hype, a distraction to the true mysteries already revealed in Christ. At worst you are a modern-day false Gnostic prophet, your fourth book on hidden mysteries has proven your first book was not really about Jesus Christ at all. You are called an apostle, you teach the Charismatic Church to bring heaven to earth, a great mystery which has been given to you alone to reveal. Sadly, real faith does not say who shall ascend into heaven, that is to bring Christ down. God has revealed Himself already in the incarnation, a great mystery revealed, God in the flesh in the person of Jesus Christ.

Colossians 2:2-4
2 That their hearts might be comforted, being knit together in love, and unto all riches of the full assurance of understanding, to the acknowledgement of the mystery of God, and of the Father, and of Christ.
3 In whom are hid all the treasures of wisdom and knowledge.
4 And this I say, lest any man should beguile you with enticing words.

Colossians 1:25-27

25 Whereof I am made a minister, according to the dispensation of God which is given to me for you, to fulfil the word of God;

26 Even the mystery which hath been hid from ages and from generations, but now is made manifest to his saints:

27 To whom God would make known what is the riches of the glory of this mystery among the Gentiles, which is Christ in you, the hope of glory:

Ephesians 3:1-6

1 For this cause I Paul, the prisoner of Jesus Christ for you Gentiles,

2 If ye have heard of the dispensation of the grace of God which is given me to you-ward:

3 How that by revelation he made known unto me the mystery; (as I wrote afore in few words,

4 Whereby, when ye read, ye may understand my knowledge in the mystery of Christ)

5 Which in other ages was not made known unto the sons of men, as it is now revealed unto his holy apostles and prophets by the Spirit.

6 That the Gentiles should be fellow heirs, and of the same body, and partakers of his promise in Christ by the gospel:

A Lying Spirit in the Prophetic

Today we have a major issue uncorrected in the Charismatic Movement of failed predictive words of prophecy. One might justify false prophecy as part of modern prophets, but never does the Bible say false prophecy comes from true prophets. If the Movement keeps on with this practice without major reforms, then its stands in error before the Lord. If God did not release false prophetic words who then is responsible?

First of all, a prophet can prophesy falsely out of the vain imaginations of his or her own heart. If a man persists to give false prophecy even after exposed, then his own flesh is giving place to sin. When you make provision for the flesh evil spirits will come to accommodate the deception you are practicing. Many who are supposed to be prophets are fallen into this deception. What is even more alarming is where a supposed prophet is hardened to correction and has become a lying spirit in the mouths of the prophets. This is even a deeper level of evil as Satan has gained a footing and functions as a lying spirit among the prophets. I believe the Prophetic Movement has fallen to a lying spirit as it has failed to correct its own error in false prophecy and doctrines.

When Gods people move into idol worship and man-made glorification the false prophets arise to give false guidance by a Satanic lying spirit. These spirits come as familiar spirits or angels of light imitating the Spirit of God in prophecy. It has become dangerous in the prophetic Movement to be around supposed prophets who are fallen to listening to lying spirits which act like the prophetic voice of God. The danger is in the seductive power these men and women function as they have been deceived to think their prophetic words and power is the Presence of God in their lives. The people in their meetings get all excited and rush into all the false prophetic, even falling down under the power which is present. Long drawn-out predictive words which the supposed prophets say they have gotten in visions or from angels, opens the audience up to receive Satan's imitation of God. Let us be clear Satan has used false prophets in Israel to lead the people to worship idols. Now New Testament false prophets which have never judged themselves and are lifted up by the people as marvelous prophet of God, have fallen into Satan's snare.

Never let a man say he speaks from God is entitled to give false lying prophecies. First of all, in the New Testament God has given the Holy Spirit to every born-again Christian. Everyone born of the Spirit is to be led of the Holy Spirit, and not to follow the Prophets like in the Old Testament. The basic function of the gift of prophecy in the New Testament is not for predicting the future. Neither is the prophetic to produce visions upon demand, or spirit travel upon demand, or travel into heaven to speak with angels. Where the Prophetic Movement has come is outside the bounds of New Testament Christianity and has become New Age in its practice. Since the New Age Movement is a form of mysticism and witchcraft, lying spirits abound in the mouths of the prophets.

Lying spirits which come from angels of light have invaded the Movement. Prophetic Charismatics now teach Christian tarot card reading, and fortune telling. Their philosophy is the New Age has been stolen from the Church so prophetic Charismatics can recover New Age practices making them Christian. Never has one prophet ever sanctified the New Age even one inch, so New Age lying spirits functions inside the Prophetic under the label of being prophetic words from the Holy Spirit. How far has the Church fallen to Satanic deception when supposed prophets and apostles cannot even discern the difference between the Holy Spirit and New Age familiar spirits, and lying spirits of prophecy? I have yet to find one single voice of the Prophetic Movement which has sounded the alarm of lying spirits, and angels of light manifesting as prophetic words from God. Yet they pride themselves in their love for God and speaking life to the Church.

How much sickness which comes from lying spirits of Satan which go unchecked inside the Movement? How long will the supposed prophets who presume to speak for God allow for their failed predictions rebuke and chasten them for being vessels of lying deception? Will this Movement now admit what may have started out as Biblical prophetic ministry and New Testament prophets has fallen to Satanic wiles and deception? When will the Prophetic Movement bring to account the false prophets in their own midst? If not, God must act and bring into account the prophets who speak lies in the name of the Lord.

2 Chronicles 18:18-26

18 Again he said, Therefore hear the word of the Lord; I saw the Lord sitting upon his throne, and all the host of heaven standing on his right hand and on his left.

19 And the Lord said, Who shall entice Ahab king of Israel, that he may go up and fall at Ramoth–gilead? And one spake saying after this manner, and another saying after that manner.

20 Then there came out a spirit, and stood before the Lord, and said, I will entice him. And the Lord said unto him, Wherewith?

21 And he said, I will go out, and be a lying spirit in the mouth of all his prophets. And the Lord said, Thou shalt entice him, and thou shalt also prevail: go out, and do even so.

22 Now therefore, behold, the Lord hath put a lying spirit in the mouth of these thy prophets, and the Lord hath spoken evil against thee.

23 Then Zedekiah the son of Chenaanah came near, and smote Micaiah upon the cheek, and said, Which way went the Spirit of the Lord from me to speak unto thee?

24 And Micaiah said, Behold, thou shalt see on that day when thou shalt go into an inner chamber to hide thyself.

25 Then the king of Israel said, Take ye Micaiah, and

carry him back to Amon the governor of the city, and to
Joash the king's son;
26 And say, Thus saith the king, Put this fellow in the
prison, and feed him with bread of affliction and with
water of affliction, until I return in peace.

Despise Not Prophesying

The apostle Paul in reproving the error of beliefs about
the Second Coming finished by saying, do not quench
the Holy Spirit, and do not despise prophesying. Prove
all things, hold fast that which is good. Abstain all
appearance of evil. The modern Church of Charismatics
have then used this passage to allow false prophesy as a
normal course of sifting out prophetic words. The
thought by rejecting prophecy you will quench the Holy
Spirit. Is this the true meaning of what quenching the
Holy Spirit really means? To accept a great deal of false
prophetic predictions for in the process a true word of
the Lord may be present.

I have a question, why wouldn't Christians despise false
Prophecy? Doesn't the admonition to test the spirits, to
prove all things then suggest Christians can know the
true from the false?
Why would the Scriptures warn of the false prophets
who work by a spirit of error, and Christians have an
anointing to overcome them? How dangerous are the
false prophecies which come from men inside the
Church? In not despising prophecy was Paul saying not

to despise false prophesy. In no way can Christians be in any agreement with false prophets, and false prophesy. Do you love a lie, even if it were to come in a form which says God showed me, or God told me? Where in Scriptures are, we told to compromise with the Spirit of truth, and accept false prophesy in order to have the true too.

This I am sure of false prophecy of any kind is not to be tolerated in fear of quenching the Spirit. As false prophesy did not originate with the Holy Spirit and has behind deep ramifications which also include evil spirits at work in the Church. Any man who gives a failed predictive word should take a serious look into their motives, and reasons to minister the word of the Lord. I am very sure Paul was not asking Christians to accept false prophecy alongside the true the way it is practiced in the modern Charismatic church of today.

Instead, Paul was asking Christians not to despise authentic prophecy. Real prophecy from the Lord in Paul's day would have likely asked Christians to endure the hardships, trails, and tests which caused great suffering in their day. So severe was the persecution of the first century Church many had thought they were in the Great Tribulation, and Caesar Nero was the Antichrist. Prophetic words were likely to encourage and exhort the saints to endure until the end. Many would suffer the loss of all things in keeping their testimony in the face of persecution and threat of martyrdom. Prophecy from the Holy Spirit was not a false prediction of politics like we hear today. So many failed Charismatics prophetic predictions come from a philosophical belief. Like making President Trump a modern-day Cyrus, and building a whole theology based upon government and politics.

If you miss a predictive word of prophecy, especially after trying to convince the Church you are a prophet of God is serious business. You have quenched the Holy Spirit by misleading the body of Christ who have foolishly put their trust in your reputation as a prophet. The Scriptures warns how false prophets will deceive the people leading many astray by great swelling words of vanity. Any time a man who claims to be a prophet of God and gives false predictions the Church should warn of serious deception and error. After all the Holy Spirit is the Spirit of Truth and would never lead anyone to speak falsely in the name of the Lord. Any supposed prophet who refused to admit deception and refuses to repent has surely grieved the Holy Spirit and will be judged by God.

1 Thessalonians 5:19-23
19 Quench not the Spirit.
20 Despise not prophesyings.
21 Prove all things; hold fast that which is good.
22 Abstain from all appearance of evil.
23 And the very God of peace sanctify you wholly; and I pray God your whole spirit and soul and body be

preserved blameless unto the coming of
our Lord Jesus Christ.

Chapter Seven
Judging Prophets and Prophecy

How To Judge Prophecy

Since the Charismatic Movement has been exposed
with giving false prophecies, why couldn't those false
prophecies have been judged before the name of the
Lord was defiled? How could any Christian know for
sure if a prophetic word has actually originated with the
Holy Spirit? What standard of measure has been given
to the Church to judge prophecies? First of all, no man is
given a right to speak in the name of the Lord by his
own private interpretations. No special revelation which
come from new interpretations of Scriptures are
allowed. This has been the major issue inside the
Charismatic Movement, private interpretations being
put as "new light" of worn-out doctrinal beliefs.
Especially in relationship to end time judgments and the
Second Coming of the Lord. Instead of preaching or
teaching doctrine about end times, the Prophetic
Movement has practiced predicting prophetically end
time events. If Charismatics could really see 99% of their
predictions are really philosophical beliefs being
prophesied in the name of the Lord. Instead of

preaching or teaching their position, Charismatics use the name of the Lord to bring credibility.

When judging prophecy, one can see if the prophecy is really a doctrinal statement as compared to a prophetic word. The Scriptures do not allow for new doctrines to spoken as prophecy, as New Testament prophecy is a gift of the Holy Spirit, and not to develop new doctrines. The Holy Spirit would never speak against what has already been written in the Word of God. The Charismatic Prophetic Movement is constantly violating this principle, by bringing in private interpretation, new revelations which cannot be supported by what is written in the Scriptures.

Here is a safety measure when testing a prophetic word. Does it violate Gods written word and will? A prophetic word should not undermine the Scriptures in any way. In judging a prophetic word, Christians should be able to point to the doctrines in the Scriptures as support and measurement. For example, prophecy would never falsely lift up a man exposing him to being glorified and idolized. Yet, many Charismatic words have been guilty of exalting a man into a position God has never intended and is rebuked by Scriptures. Man-made wisdom and glorification is often put off as a prophetic word and can be easily discerned as coming from a man's flesh, and not the Holy Spirit gift of prophecy.

The gift of prophecy as written in Scriptures is a word spoken by inspiration of the Holy Spirit, for edification, exhortation, and comfort. When the Prophetic Movement attempted to go beyond the Biblical gift of prophecy, a false practice was introduced and normalized. Instead of the gift of prophecy, supernatural experiences were substituted. These manifestations were labeled as the "extreme prophetic," and introduced New Age spirituality into the Charismatic Prophetic Movement. In fact, the major leaders of the Prophetic Movement have taught the New Age was stolen from the Church and must be recovered. Now days the false prophetic includes Charismatics using tarot cards and predicting the future. Instead of the gift of prophecy psychic manifestations coming from soul power are now called words of prophecy.

As New Age is a form of witchcraft using soul powers, as the result evil spirits have invaded the Prophetic Movement. Today, a Charismatic might be taught New Age practices like spirit travel, where a man can leave his body and travel by his spirit. Others might teach how to travel by mystical portals into heaven. Communication with the dead, and angels, and visions upon demand all have tapped into psychic and New Age powers. All these manifestations are labeled a prophetic ministry, and all manner of lying dreams, visions, and angels of light have invaded the Movement. Without restraint from the true gift of prophecy, and the Written Word of God, the Prophetic Movement has become a haven of deception and error as demonstrated by the hundreds of false and lying predictions which have exposed their prophets.

Until the standard of Scriptures is restored the true gift of prophecy will be lost to demonic counterfeits being passed off as the Word of the Lord.

Suppose you have common knowledge about situations, in which a great deal of people already know about. Then you have a dream about that situation, or feel God wants you to speak about those know facts. I have a choice, I can just talk about it without trying to "make it a prophet word," instead just speaking about my concerns in a typical teaching, preaching, or common communication way. If I wanted people to identify me "as a prophet," and I was always needing to "give a prophetic word," I can take what is known by common knowledge and put a "thus says the Lord," upon what I am saying. By doing this it leads the Church to believe the word I am speaking has come by revelation knowledge. What am I really doing, I want to be known as a prophet, and I am subtlety "marketing my gifting," so I can gain acceptance as a prophet whom God speaks through, and gain an audience? Of course, this is selfish ambition, and misuse of the prophetic gifting, by self-promotion.

Let me give you an example. It has over the years been commonly known within the black churches, sometimes Church leaders have suffered with sexual immorality. Not that other Churches, like white Churches do not have the same problems. Instead, black Churches have gained "a reputation for sexual immorality," as a problem with some black leadership. Now of course this can "really play into racial prejudice," as sexual immorality is not a race problem, instead it is a human nature sin problem. So, if I have gained a reputation as a prophet, and I say God showed me in Black Churches judgment has come because of the all the immorality among black leaders, I might just be stirring up a big racial divide. Especially if I am a white guy "prophet," who somehow "has overlooked" some of the same issues going on in white Churches.

For example, I might also say "God has showed me," in black Churches leadership is set up to be idolized by Church members. I say God is judging this idolatry, and abuse of powers, especially in the area of financial exploitation. Where black Church leaders are guilty of lording over the peoples for "personal profit, a spirit of mammon. However, as a "white prophet," my white friends in ministry are "guilty of the same exploitation" over "white congregations," yet "God has not shown me prophetically," to confront the white leaders for the same idolatry, and profiteering. Why as a white prophet, would I overlook my ministry friends, and not correct them for the same sins? The simple truth is, if I

confront and correct my own ministry associations, I risk
losing those relationships, ministry platforms, and
financial opportunity. I overlook the sins of my friends,
because it represents personal loss and cost to my
prophetic ministry and popularity.

Now what if I did not "attach a God has shown me
label," to the very same correction? Instead, I just warn
the leaders about the cost of immorality, idolatry of
ministry, and exploitation of the Church for personal
profit? It is no longer a black, or white issue, just a sin
issue. I do not have the same wight of authority, in the
eyes of the people. Even though its correct to confront
sin, leaders can they just say, it is your own personal
opinion, and I do not agree. Now, it is no longer a
prophetic word, or the weight of a prophet, instead it is
a Christian leader bringing correction. It keeps the racial
issue out of it, and the misuse of labeling it as a
prophetic judgement. Simply put you do not need to be
a prophet in the Church to confront and correct sin.
Also, you can be sure, God is judging immorality, pride,
greed, and idolatry of ministry in all of the Church.

What is the problem with the prophetic ministry today?
The pressure to preform and give prophetic words to
demonstrate you are a prophet. So many words which
are given as a word of the Lord, have behind them
ministry ambition and promotion. Just look at all the
prophets who want to sell the revelations, in some kind
of platform, or marketing, or bestselling books. I would

say any Christian who is always identifying as a prophet is off center to begin with, as their identity is in Christ, not in their ministry. I have seen this corruption for years in the prophetic and have participated in the sin and flesh through my own ministry. It is time for the prophets to see the marketing of revelation, the mysteries and secrets of God has drawn you away and into exploiting the Church "in the name of God."

1 Corinthians 14:29-40
29 Let the prophets speak two or three, and let the other judge.
30 If any thing be revealed to another that sitteth by, let the first hold his peace.
31 For ye may all prophesy one by one, that all may learn, and all may be comforted.
32 And the spirits of the prophets are subject to the prophets.
33 For God is not the author of confusion, but of peace, as in all churches of the saints.
34 Let your women keep silence in the churches: for it is not permitted unto them to speak; but they are commanded to be under obedience, as also saith the law.
35 And if they will learn any thing, let them ask their husbands at home: for it is a shame for women to speak in the church.
36 What? came the word of God out from you? or came it unto you only?

37 If any man think himself to be a prophet, or spiritual, let him acknowledge that the things that I write unto you are the commandments of the Lord.
38 But if any man be ignorant, let him be ignorant.
39 Wherefore, brethren, covet to prophesy, and forbid not to speak with tongues.
40 Let all things be done decently and in order.

Judging Annual Predictive Prophetic Words

Since 2020 exposed the false predictions from the Charismatic prophets, are we now to trust their 2021 predictions? From common sense I would think this will be a very difficult year with a change in the Presidency, and a socialism being adopted. Even if President Trump were to somehow overthrow the election results, a civil war would break with a great deal of violence.

The New administration has vowed to close down the economy for several months fighting the Coronavirus pandemic which will bankrupt a considerable number of small businesses. Just using the facts as they exist right now would lend towards a very difficult economic year. Also, the new administration is pro-Islamic and has proven to be not very sympathetic towards Christian morality and beliefs. It could be a very difficult year for the Church as new laws are legislated which limit the freedom of worship. The point being I can use common sense to see where things might be headed without playing God and attaching the name of the Lord to what

I think. In the process of walking out the year I might have a dream which confirms what I have already reasoned to be true. Should I then exploit the Church with all manner of declaring predictive prophetic words?

What is wrong with this practice? It is obvious my beliefs would influence the way I judge supposed prophetic revelations. For example, if I believe in the 7 Mountain mandate to take over the world by cleansing the 7 pillars of culture, I am already colored with an expectation. This was a major issue with false prophecy in 2020, as the supposed prophets attached the 7 Mountain mandate to President Trump. Every predictive prophetic word was about Trump cleansing the system and bringing revival to the nations. The predetermined result was put into prophetic words, all of which failed horribly as the nation was at values war for the four years of the Trump Presidency. 2020 exposed the prophet's ideology's which were being manipulated into predictive prophetic words. 2020 exposed the hypocrisy of false prophecy and brought it right out into the open where everyone could see the deception. The problem is the prophets acted like it was the first time they gave a false prophecy. The reality is this was a culmination of years even decades of false prophecy. The prophets have pushed an agenda in the name of God which cannot be found in the Scriptures.

We do not need prophets to predict the future for us. Neither do we need the prophets to direct the Church through prophecy. As every born-again Christian is given the Holy Spirit to lead and guide the Church. Prophets do not function like Old Testament prophets in predicting the future, as every Christian is directed by God Himself. What has been the danger, a spirit of error in the prophets attempting to function like Old Testament prophets with practicing future telling. Are the prophets more capable than the Spirit of God in leading the Church into all truth? We can see the Holy Spirit direct Christians to the person of Jesus Christ, where the prophets have directed Christians to depended on their ministries. Unless the prophets keep giving their private revelations, they will lose their audience. In this way they practice seduction using the carrot of predictive prophetic words to keep their audience engaged and committed.

What are New Testament prophets really to do? All the examples of prophets in the New Testament like Peter, Paul, John, and others used the Gospel to confront the Church. Preach the word, be urgent in season and out of season reprove, rebuke, exhort with all long suffering and doctrine. The prophets who received the revelations of Jesus Christ were taught the doctrines of Christ and committed their entire lives to preaching and teaching those doctrines.

They did not add to those revelations their own personal interpretations, or subjective revelations. The prophets of the New Testament warned continuously against men adding or subtracting from the revelations already given by Jesus Christ. In this way the prophets of God were able to develop the Church. Th function of the prophets is to bring the Church into Christ likeness and maturity.

When prophecy is substituted as the word of God, the very opposite happens. Personal interpretations are given as the Word of God and the Church is brought under bondage. A great deception has taken hold of the prophetic ministry for these very practices. 2021 will be a year of reckoning for these Charismatic prophets. Will they continue in their hypocrisy as if nothing has happened? Or will they judge themselves before God acts with a greater degree of rebuke?

Ephesians 4:11-16
11 And he gave some, apostles; and some, prophets; an d some, evangelists; and some, pastors andteachers;
12 For the perfecting of the saints, for the work of the ministry, for the edifying of the body of Christ:
13 Till we all come in the unity of the faith, and of the knowledge of the Son of God, unto perfect man, unto the measure of the stature of the fulness of Christ:
14 That we henceforth be no more children, tossed to and fro, and carried about with every wind of

doctrine, by the sleight of men, and cunning
craftiness, whereby they lie in wait to deceive;
15 But speaking the truth in love, may grow
up into him in all things, which is the head, even Christ:
16 From whom the whole body fitly joined
together and compacted by that
which every joint supplieth, according to the effectual
working in the measure of
every part, maketh increase of the body unto the
edifying of itself in love.

How Dangerous Is False Prophecy

First of all, the New Testament gift of prophecy has not
supernatural details in it, its basic function is
exhortation, edification, and comfort. In this way when
inspired by the Holy Spirit, prophecy helps strengthen
and encourage the body of Christ. Also, in this way the
simple gift has no future predictions, or present-day
facts which could be false information. Prophecy often
serves as the clothing for other gifts of the Spirit which
can function along with the simple gift of prophecy.
When details of the future are added, it is still prophecy
but has an added dimension of future prediction, or
words of wisdom. The word of wisdom given by the
Holy Spirit is considered a revolutionary gift, and by
itself is not considered prophecy. Instead of future
prediction, the word of knowledge can reveal present
day facts, or past history in supernatural details without

prior knowledge. This also is considered a Holy Spirit gift of revelation and is no considered prophecy by itself. However, words of wisdom and knowledge can be combined with a word of prophecy giving future details, or words of knowledge giving present day facts or past history. This is where the problem with the prophetic has happened over the past 20 years. The gift of prophecy was pushed aside, and supernatural revelation was put in its place. All manner of visions, dreams, angelic encounters, and spirit travel are now considered prophecy.

What is now the major problem with prophetic words? The revelations being given are not prophecy, they are standalone predictions of the future. Or stand-alone revelations from angels, or visions. As revelation is become what the Charismatic Movement calls the prophetic, it must be "tested weighed and measured," as to true or false right or wrong. Not just that, but also its origin, did it come from the Holy Spirit, and does it stand up to what has already been written in the Word pf God? The simple gift or prophecy is easy to judge as its just exhortative in nature. Revelation of the other hand can be very dangerous, as we have already experienced in the Prophetic Movement. When a false prophetic prediction is given, it fails the test of origin, it did not come from the Holy Spirit. It also has failed the test of truth, being a lie, and it violated the testimony of

Jesus the Spirit of Prophecy which means the person has given a false witness in the name of God.

Giving lying false witness in the name of God is dangerous. Think about it you speak against God, which puts you in judgment with God. Your personal subject revelations are being put against what God has spoken in His infallibility. You are tempting men with a seduction to disobey Gods infallible words and follow your personal subjective revelations. You are creating a following based upon your subjective revelations which moves those who follow away from the Lord, and after you. Your subjective revelations are creating a division, a schisms in the Church, where Christians must put your private interpretations before the infallible Word of God. How dangerous you have become when men follow your subject revelations, and private interpretations, above the authority of Gods written infallible Word.

You might consider you false predictions just an error in judgment. You give yourself a lot of latitude to keep on making these false predictions, as you have created a ministry following for yourself. In every measure of judgment, you are found guilty of being a false witness. Your insistence to keep giving private subjective revelations in God's name has made you danger. You are blinded by your own desires, and you stand opposed to God. The Lord might likely confront you with the voice of an ass, or just by the confrontation of Christians outside you sphere of influence. If you do not take heed, your judgment and damnable heresies will bring you to an unlikely end. As God must judge you as a false witness, and your false predictions as the actions of a false prophet. Whose judgment lingers not, and whose damnation does not slumber.

2 Peter
But there were false prophets also among the people, even as there shall be false teachers among you, who privily shall bring in damnable heresies, even denying the Lord that bought them, and bring upon themselves swift destruction.
2 And many shall follow their pernicious ways; by reason of whom the way of truth shall be evil spoken of.
3 And through covetousness shall they with feigned words make merchandise of you: whose judgment now of a long time lingereth not, and their damnation slumbereth not.

Chapter Eight
Psychic Words of Prophecy

In recent meeting a Charismatic prophet was supposedly receiving Words of prophecy, began to see dead relatives in heaven and pass messages to the living relatives in the meeting. Why was no Charismatic in the room questioning the practice of a psychic medium like behavior?

First of all, for years this very same group has been trained in the recovery of the New Age Movement inside the Church. Second, the authority of Scriptures has been vastly reduced in the eyes of these Charismatics who have been taught supernatural experiences are the final source of validity. Just as long as you are sincere and genuinely seeking God, no real deception can come your way. Anyone who questions the source of the supernatural is just not open to heaven being brought to earth by these supernatural experiences. In their minds the veil between heaven and earth had grown so thin, this Charismatic prophet was able to see into heaven and communicate with the dead.

However, just saying you see their dead relative is one thing but getting Christians to follow along with your deception is quite a different matter. So how did the prophet get such a dramatic response? Supernatural details were given which if fact were accurate and treated as supernatural Holy Spirit revelation. He gave some birth dates, or some death dates, some names of dead relatives, or names of living relatives. Many times, the prophet would just call out the person by name, giving their birth dates, or anniversary dates, or their physical house address. Now with those details being given by supernatural knowledge, must also be supernaturally given by God. In essence supernatural facts given by the prophet acting as a medium, in a Christian meeting made this New Age practice acceptable.

However, one must question are Christian prophets the only one who can get names and addresses supernaturally? The answer should not be surprising, as this practice is most often found around New Age and occult psychics. In fact, supernatural revelation is what gives the Psychic credibility before his audience. Evidence like names and birth dates, in fact prove contact with a dead relative is legitimate.

Now does God who has given the Holy Spirit to every Born-Again believer, and the right and privilege to boldly approach the Throne of God on the basis of the Cross, need a prophet to speak to the living on behalf of the dead? Does God need to validate life after death by giving visions of dead relatives, so they can report through the prophet they made it to heaven, and all is well?

Where in Scriptures do, we see the prophets of God getting personal information no matter how accurate, to speak with the dead-on behalf of the living. So why did no Charismatics question the practice as occult in origin? Why would no Christian confront the prophet, as being guided by psychic ability, or demonic spirits called familiar spirits of fortune telling? Instead of seeing the grave danger and practice many received their messages from their dead relatives, like coming from dead fathers, mothers, or children. Supernatural psychic ability was opening the door for a false intimacy with God and was being imitated by familiar spirits. Relatives who received the supernatural communication of necromancy began to weep. Why because they were afraid of deception, absolutely not. Instead, the supernatural details gave them confidence the New Age prophet was in fact acting as a medium between them and their dead relatives in heaven.

Now is this the practice of the Christian faith, the function of a New Testament prophet, or the proper use of the New Testament gift of prophecy? The answer is absolutely not, it is demonic New Age witchcraft and occultism. Are the facts really supernatural, names, addresses, and birth dates real, of course that is what convinces Charismatics their experience is authentic. Is the source then the Holy Spirit because the details are so accurate? The answer is absolutely not, its source and origin is psychic ability, soul power, familiar spirits, or both. Evil spirits who have convinced the prophet he is hearing the voice of God. However, without the Bible as the standard of final authority, the practice of being a New Age medium, or the practice of Necromancy goes without challenge.

What Is Soul Power

At this time, it would be good to define physic ability. Resident in every man is the portion of his life called the soul. It is the immaterial part of the man which comprises his mind, will and emotion. Sometimes the soul of man can be identified as the personality of the man, that part which makes him a unique individual. Now with psychic ability the powers of the soul are developed to perform functions which are not normally practiced in normal everyday communications.

For example, the ability to read another person's mind or communicate by projecting mental thoughts is called the psychic ability of Telepathy. How then can mind reading, and casting your thoughts into the mind of another person happen? That ability is created by practice, by opening up your soul to the possibility. Seeking to break down natural human limits which confine the soul. In effect you are breaking down your soul, so you can introduce supernatural abilities like moving objects or bending objects with your mind, Telekinesis. So, an adept has broken down the soul, and has developed his soul powers can operate in supernatural abilities which in fact are psychic soul power. So many Christians who are pursuing supernatural manifestations have failed to understand the laws which govern man to keep proper limits and boundaries, keeping protective measures in place. In this way New Age Psychic ability and soul power is often mistaken for the supernatural work of the Holy Spirit.

A Charismatic Christian who is constantly pursuing prophetic encounters and words from God can open up his soul powers thinking they are the work of the Holy Spirit. This kind of prophetic person is feeling constantly compelled to give prophetic words to those who they are around. They are pushed to speak a word of prediction or prophecy as the feeling is strong inside their soul. They have failed to recognize prophetic words which come from the Holy Spirit originate from inside the human spirit. The Holy Spirit working inside the Born-Again human spirit, to give inspiration, a word of prophecy, only as the Holy Spirit leads. So, no compulsion and push from soul power compels the person to give a prophecy. Instead, the spirit of the prophet are subject to the prophet, under his control, not forced or pushed or feeling compelled to always prophecy or give prophetic predictions.

1 Corinthians 14:29-33
29 Let the prophets speak two or three, and let the other judge.
30 If anything be revealed to another that sitteth by, let the first hold his peace.
31 For ye may all prophesy one by one, that all may learn, and all may be comforted.
32 And the spirits of the prophets are subject to the prophets.
33 For God is not the author of confusion, but of peace, as in all churches of the saints.

Quote from Watchman Nee

"We are now drawing nearer to the time of great apostasy. "The momentum is increasing rapidly," observed Mrs. Penn-Lewis. "The hand of the Arch enemy of God and man is on the helm, and the world is rushing to the dark hour, when, for a brief period, Satan will actually be the 'god of this age', ruling through a superman whose 'parousia' (appearance) cannot long be delayed."* What is soul power? By going to the Scriptures and under the illumination of the Holy Spirit believers ought to realize that this power is so hellish as to spread over all nations on earth and to turn the whole world into chaos.

Satan is now engaging this soul power to serve as a substitute for God's gospel and its power. He tries to blind people's hearts, through the marvel of soul force, into accepting a bloodless religion. He also uses the discoveries of psychic sciences to cast doubt upon the value of supernatural occurrences in Christianity— causing people to consider the latter as likewise being nothing but the latent power of the soul. He aims at substituting Christ's salvation with psychic force. The modern attempt to change evil habits and bad temperaments by hypnosis is a forerunner to this objective.

The children of God can be protected only by knowing the difference between spirit and soul. If the deeper work of the cross is not applied to our Adamic life and by the Holy Spirit a real-life union is affected with the

Resurrected Lord, we may unwittingly develop our soul power.
Watchman Nee; Latent Power of the Soul pg. 26

New Age Influences

A question needs to be asked concerning false prophetic predictions. Are New Age influences the invading Prophetic Movement? I want to give 5 points where false doctrines demonstrate this fact:

1) Jesus Christ Is Just a Man:
2) Man is Basically Good:
3) The World Is Getting Better All the Time:
4) Utopian Society:
5) Church Will Save the World:

Before I expose the Charismatic heresy of denying the incarnation by saying Jesus Christ is just a man and not God. First, I want to break down the danger in point two: Man is basically good Charismatic teaching and how it plays into the New Age. Of course, the whole emphasis in New Age beliefs is where man evolves into his "better self." The whole concept of transcendence of man becoming, the evolution of man into the divine self, is part of New Age beliefs. So, society which refuses to acknowledge the "sin nature," is always looking for man to repair culture, and save the world. The whole concept of a better man than what has existed before, is moving the world to an Age of Aquarius, a golden age where man evolves, and world peace is obtained.

Now many Charismatic apostles are attempting to sell the Church a belief the man is basically good. In fact, some have pushed the heresy man is not born alienated from God and there is no original sin. Some Charismatic teachers attack the doctrine of Jesus Christ dying as our sin substitute, instead teaching Jesus Christ died to restore our relationship with God. Next you will hear how the world is improving all the time, and the most powerful Church the world will ever experience is happening now and in the near future. In fact, one Charismatic apostle is so convinced on a golden age of the Church (Age of Aquarius) teaches the Church is in the New Heavens and Earth right now and the first resurrection as "already assumed come to past." In this way we can see the Prophetic Movement is susceptible to New Age beliefs with Christian terminology attempting to make it acceptable.

Now what is the real danger when the New Age, Golden Age, of evolving man is packaged with Christian terminology? The push is away from any real recognition of the sinfulness of man. How sin has corrupted this present evil age, and how fallen man is a natural enemy to God. Is the nature of man changed since the fall of Adam in the Garden of God? Can you dress up a pig in nice cloths put some nice perfume, so it does not stink, and declare it has evolved, has become a more sophisticated pig? Put that pig back into its pen, and what will the pretty pig do he does so by nature, going back to wallowing in the mud. Making things better on the outside of a man like his environment does not change the inside of a man, he is still by nature a child of God's wrath. That is why the modern Charismatic prophets rarely preaches the Cross, or addresses sin in the Church, or teaches on the demonic nature of the Kingdoms of this present evil age. It would be in complete contradiction to a better man, a better world, and a cultural transform gospel. In these days young people who have grown up in the Charismatic Prophetic Movement are taught the gospel of the kingdom which saves the world by transforming culture. They have no idea this Cross less gospel is based upon "the evolution of man into a better world belief." A false Charismatic Gospel which must transform the culture of nations before Jesus Christ can return. Eerily similar to New Age beliefs.

Now these Charismatic apostles and prophets are deceiving the younger generation of Christians by teaching the need to recover what the New Age stole from the Church? In the future when you meet a Charismatic mentored young person who will think you have "no faith, or even a sin conscience," Any belief in a great apostasy or falling away from the faith will have no place in their philosophical beliefs. if you confront them about their need to repent from their sins and rebellion of Jesus Chris, they might think you have a religious spirit. Sadly, Christian foundations will have been eroded leading to no real understanding of the Blood Sacrifice of Jesus Christ on the Cross. A true undermining of the Cross by New Age influences.

We are on the verge of seeing some of the most Bible ignorant New Age like Charismatic Christians the Charismatic Church has ever developed. Charismatics who are attempting to save the world, speaking words of prophetic destiny over the unsaved without any gospel presentation. Charismatics who pray for New Age like mystical signs and wonders, and attempt to travel into heaven on demand, talk with angels and seek spirit guides. All New Age practices which are now being adopted into the Christian faith. New Age practices forbidden by Scriptures like communicating with the dead, passing messages from the dead saints in heaven like Elijah or some other well know Bible person. All these New Age practices adopted into the Prophetic Movement done by training and activation in Charismatic prophetic meetings.

1Corinthians 1:17-31

17 For Christ sent me not to baptize, but to preach the gospel: not with wisdom of words, lest the cross of Christ should be made of none effect.
18 For the preaching of the cross is to them that perish foolishness; but unto us which are saved it is the power of God.
19 For it is written, I will destroy the wisdom of the

wise, and will bring to nothing the understanding of the prudent.

20 Where is the wise? where is the scribe? where is the disputer of this world? hath not God made foolish the wisdom of this world?

21 For after that in the wisdom of God the world by wisdom knew not God, it pleased God by the foolishness of preaching to save them that believe.

22 For the Jews require a sign, and the Greeks seek after wisdom:

23 But we preach Christ crucified, unto the Jews a stumbling block, and unto the Greeks foolishness;

24 But unto them which are called, both Jews and Greeks, Christ the power of God, and the wisdom of God.

25 Because the foolishness of God is wiser than men; and the weakness of God is stronger than men.

26 For ye see your calling, brethren, how that not many wise men after the flesh, not many mighty, not many noble, are called:

27 But God hath chosen the foolish things of the world to confound the wise; and God hath chosen the weak things of the world to confound the things which are mighty;

28 And base things of the world, and things which are despised, hath God chosen, yea, and things which are not, to bring to nought things that are:

29 That no flesh should glory in his presence.

30 But of him are ye in Christ Jesus, who of God is made unto us wisdom, and righteousness, and sanctification, and redemption:

31 That, according as it is written, He that glorieth, let him glory in the Lord.

Charismatics Who Deny the Incarnation

In the Christian faith the whole of its validity, its truthfulness lies in the fact God was made flesh and dwelt among us. How great is this mystery, and perhaps the greatest stumbling block to this present day even among Christians? Today in the Charismatic Movement it has become all about spiritual experiences, none of which need to be connected to the historic Jesus Christ. For you see, the Holy Spirit never works independently of the body and blood of Jesus Christ. Since our eternal redemption is all based upon the body of Jesus Christ as the Sacrificial Lamb, for all eternity faith in God requires faith in the incarnation of God. God did not save sinful man on the basis of "spirit," instead a body was prepared in which the eternal Son of God would live, die, be resurrected, and be glorified as man at the right hand of God. God will not come back in spirit, instead will come back in body as the Glorified God/Man who has been raised from the dead. The false doctrine of Manifested Sons of God which says Jesus Christ will first return through the "Church's body," is an outright denial of the body Christ who will truly come with, His own glorified body.

There has come an immense counterfeit Christianity by the denial of the incarnation where many Charismatics have denied Jesus Christ is God. It has been fine to declare Jesus Christ is God from eternity past, and Jesus Christ is God from eternity future, but not God in the incarnation. One of the great lies spoken is Jesus Christ laid aside His divinity, and only was a man in right relationship with God, and not God in the flesh. A false "mediation is implied" that Christ not being God has opened the way for the Church to bring heaven to earth and make the world Christian. Another false premise is the Church is in the process of becoming divine, and before the Second Coming of Jesus Christ will "be in equal proportion of the divine with its head Jesus Christ. All this counterfeit Christianity is the result of the denial of God in the flesh, as the only means of God connecting heaven and earth in redemption.

Here is an amazing fact, it is not spirit which redeems the fallen creation, instead a body which the eternal Son of God was born as a man. The Scriptures are clear, not the body of born-again believers, instead the body of only one man, Jesus Christ God in the flesh stands as our mediator. For there is only one mediator between God and man, the man Christ Jesus.

The Church's fake mediation of saving the world by a false Gospel, a denial of the body of Christ by denying God came in the flesh. Spirit is the false Gospel of our day, angels, heaven, dead saints, visions, dreams, prophetic predictions are all the rage of "spirituality." However, grand, and exciting these may appear, none have the basis of Mediation and cannot change the world "even one inch." For without the body and blood of God incarnated Christianity is the biggest sham the world has ever encountered. For without God becoming man being made sin for us, dying on the Cross, being resided from the dead, our faith is in vain, and we are still dead in our sins.

Makes you wonder why the Charismatics have denied the incarnation and have gone off into teaching the Church brings heaven to earth by "spirit." However, the true Christian faith speaks this way, do not say who will go into heaven for us, or who will go into Hell," but the word of faith God did all this in one body of the Lord Jesus Christ. Now in Christ alone is salvation, and no other "spirit, or body."

Hebrews 10:7-10

7 Then said I, Lo, I come (in the volume of the book it is written of me,) to do thy will, O God.
8 Above when he said, Sacrifice and offering and burnt offerings and offering for sin thou wouldest
not, neither hadst pleasure therein; which are

offered by the law;
9 Then said he, Lo, I come to do thy will, O God. He taketh away the first, that he may establish the second.
10 By the which will we are sanctified through the offering of the body of Jesus Christ once for all.

Romans 10:6-11

6 But the righteousness which is of faith speaketh on this wise, Say not in thine heart, Who shall ascend into heaven? (that is, to bring Christ down from above:)
7 Or, Who shall descend into the deep? (that is, to bring up Christ again from the dead.)
8 But what saith it? The word is nigh thee, even in thy mouth, and in thy heart: t hat is, the word of faith, which we preach;
9 That if thou shalt confess with thy mouth the Lord Jesus, and shalt believe in thine heart that God hath him from the dead, thou shalt be saved.
10 For with the heart man believeth unto righteousness; and with the mouth confession is made unto salvation.
11 For the scripture saith, Whosoever believeth on him shall not be ashamed.

The Body and Blood of Jesus Christ

It must be a man who will rule the world. In the ruling by men two types are presented 1) In Christ, and 2) in Adam. Right now, those who are in power who rule the nations are men in Adam. Which demonstrates the Cross of Jesus Christ did not give Adams lost dominion to the Church to rule over the earth as many Charismatics insist. Which leads us to the coming Son of Perdition who will come as the worlds false Messiah to rule over the world. This is Adams highest ideal, man who claims to be God, just like Satan offered Adam in the Garden. For in the day, you eat there of your eyes will be opened and you shall be gods. The Adamic principle is for man to rule the world as His own God.

Now what of Christ? Jesus did not come by water only; Jesus came by a natural birth and by a spiritual birth both related to His body. Jesus came both by water and by blood. Born of a woman, and by death and resurrection came into new life (resurrection) by the shedding of His blood. In Adam men can only rule out of their fallen nature what bodies they were born with. In Christ, men will rule out of their immortal eternal nature, including their resurrected bodies. All this right of rule came as the result of the body and blood of Jesus Christ. Perhaps the Church has been slow to understand the significance of the Resurrection, both Christs and ours.

1 John 5:6

⁶ This is he that came by water and blood, even Jesus Christ; not by water only, but by water and blood. And it is the Spirit that beareth witness because the Spirit is truth.

The truth of the Christian faith is established entirely upon "the incarnation of Jesus Christ." Without the body and blood of the incarnated eternal Son of God, mankind would never really ever have complete dominion. The Charismatic Church has fallen to a False Gospel attempting to rule the world without our resurrection into immortality. However, in the incarnation Jesus Christ came as our Mediator, one whose body was without spot or blemish. A perfect man without sin, or a sin nature. Jesus Christ born as a man was born of a Virgin, revealing God is the Father not man. The Incarnation demonstrates Jesus Christ possessed two natures in one body. Jesus Christ born 100% man, and 100% God.

When did Jesus Christ obtain the right to rule over the earth? By His virgin birth? Or by His resurrection from out among the dead? The Scriptures teach Christ obtained the Throne by presenting His body a Blood Sacrifice, and by death. Jesus Christ the only man to conquer sin and death and raised from the dead having the Keys of death and Hell. Upon His Resurrection was Jesus Christ declared the right to rule with a Scepter of Righteousness.

Hebrews 1:5-9

[5] For unto which of the angels said he at any time, Thou art my Son, this day have I begotten thee? And again, I will be to him a Father, and he shall be to me a Son?[6] And again, when he bringeth in the first begotten into the world, he saith, And let all the angels of God worship him.[7] And of the angels he saith, Who maketh his angels' spirits, and his ministers a flame of fire. [8] But unto the Son he saith, Thy throne, O God, is for ever and ever: a sceptre of righteousness is the sceptre of thy kingdom. [9] Thou hast loved righteousness, and hated iniquity; therefore God, even thy God, hath anointed thee with the oil of gladness above thy fellows.

Without Christs incarnation there would be no sinless spotless Lamb of God who takes away the sins of the world. Without the body of Jesus Christ and the shedding of blood there would be no redemption of mankind from sin and death. Without the resurrection of Jesus Christ there would be no dominion over Satan and death. Without our resurrection Christians could never rule the nations with the Lord Jesus Christ. For it is impossible for flesh and blood to inherit the Kingdom of God, neither can a man with a corrupt nature rule with Christ in the first resurrection.

1 Corinthians 15:50

[50] Now this I say, brethren, that flesh and blood cannot inherit the kingdom of God; neither doth corruption inherit incorruption.

Now Jesus Christ will take rule in the Kingdom of heaven at the Second Coming when He comes to take possession of the earth. Forever since the incarnation, the Cross, the Resurrection, Christ has become man. Jesus Christ will from that time rule the heavens and the earth as the Glorified Resurrected Eternal Son of God, while still fully a man.

The body and blood of Jesus Christ have given us the one and only King of Kings and Lord of Lords.

Major Charismatic False Prophecy: Christ Will Only Return For A Glorious Church

Have you repeatedly heard Jesus Christ will not "return for a dirty bride?" He will only come for a glorious Church without spot or wrinkle. To prophecy God will only come after the Church has become glorious in this age might be the most often spoken false prophecy of the Charismatic Movement. The philosophical beliefs which surround Charismatics concerning a glorious end time Church has fueled the fires of thousands false prophecies. Has raised up a deluge of false prophets who are constantly predicting how a coming new breed of Christians will overtake the world with God's glory. Not as the Church exists now, sin ridden, worldly, powerless, unbelieving, a future Church with great glory and miracles to make the world Christian.

So, will Jesus Christ not return for a dirty, sin ridden, unbelieving Church? This is a crucial question as many Christians are following men who say they "can make the Church glorious." Sad to say the Church in this present evil age will "always be defiled by sin and evil spirits." The Church in this age is marked by its mixture of true and false. The kingdom parable of the Wheat and Tares proves Jesus Christ returns when the height of true and false are at its greatest. Where the wheat the sons of God are putting on the full head of grain, and the tares the sons of the evil one are also come into fruition. Only at the Second Coming will Jesus Christ separate out the Wheat from the Tares. It is at the Second Coming Christ will present to Himself the 5 Chaste Virgins who qualify as the Bride of Christ. To the other 5 Virgins will be shut out from the Marriage Supper of the Lamb. For not all Christians have prepared themselves to be part of the Bridal Company.

Is the modern Church a filthy Bride now? The Church is deep into sin and deception right now just as the Scriptures has warned. For in the last days many shall depart from the faith giving heed to seducing spirits and doctrines of demons. (1 Timothy 4:1) Will a new breed of leaders lead the Church out of darkness? On the contrary evil men and imposters will wax worse and worse in the Church deceiving and being deceived.

Instead of a new breed of apostolic leaders, or true prophets the Church will be overrun by seducers who lead the Church into apostasy teachings doctrines of demons instead of the doctrines of Jesus Christ. (2 Timothy 3:13) Will the Church escape all this end time deception becoming a glorious Church without spot? Or does the Bible warn of perilous times before the Second Coming? Yes, perilous times are warned where the character of Christ is removed from the Church by corrupted leaders. A sin laden Church holding to a form of godliness without the character of Christ.

Are modern Christians in the time of peril from evil spirits who have access to the Church through deceived leaders who teach doctrines of demons? Perhaps the new breed will lead the Church out of the false Gospel into "new hidden mysteries which they have special privilege to access" by this secret knowledge will lead Church into great glory. Actually, the opposite happens, for in the last days Christians will turn to fables rejecting the true Gospel heaping to themselves teachers according to their lusts who will itch their ears telling them what they want to hear. (Timothy 4:1-4)

The Scriptures actually warn of end time apostasy and not a glorious end time Church. What if modern day apostles and prophets reject the council of an end time apostasy ? Can their teachings and prophecy then transform the Church into glory? The answer is simple. They only deceive themselves and others. As the reject the authority of Scriptures and rewrite what the Bible says. In this way they have become the false prophets warned of by Scriptures. Flooding the Church with volumes of false prophecies of a Glories End time Church which will never happen in this present evil age.

2 Thessalonians 2:1-17

1 Now we beseech you, brethren, by the coming of our Lord Jesus Christ, and by our gathering together unto him,

2 That ye be not soon shaken in mind, or be troubled, neither by spirit, nor by word, nor by letter as from us, as that the day of Christ is at hand.

3 Let no man deceive you by any means: for that day shall not come, except there come a falling away first, and that man of sin be revealed, the son of perdition;

4 Who opposeth and exalteth himself above all that is called God, or that is worshipped; so that he as God sitteth in the temple of God, shewing himself that he is God.

5 Remember ye not, that, when I was yet with you, I told you these things?

6 And now ye know what withholdeth that he might be revealed in his time.

7 For the mystery of iniquity doth already work: only he who now letteth will let, until he be taken out of the way.

8 And then shall that Wicked be revealed, whom the Lord shall consume with the spirit of his mouth, and shall destroy with the brightness of his coming:

9 Even him, whose coming is after the working of Satan with all power and signs and lying wonders,

10 And with all deceivableness of unrighteousness in them that perish; because they received not the love of the truth, that they might be saved.

11 And for this cause God shall send them strong delusion, that they should believe a lie:

12 That they all might be damned who believed not the truth but had pleasure in unrighteousness.

13 But we are bound to give thanks alway to God for you, brethren beloved of the Lord, because God hath from the beginning chosen you to salvation through sanctification of the Spirit and belief of the truth:

14 Whereunto he called you by our gospel, to the obtaining of the glory of our Lord Jesus Christ.15 Therefore, brethren, stand fast, and hold the traditions which ye have been taught, whether by word, or our epistle.

 6 Now our Lord Jesus Christ himself, and God, even our Father, which hath loved us, and hath given us everlasting consolation and good hope through grace,

17 Comfort your hearts and stablish you in every good word and work.

Is the Church Preparing the Way for Christ or Antichrist

In these days, the question of the condition of modern organized Christianity must be addressed. As the Scriptures warn in the last days many will depart from the faith giving heed to seducing spirits and doctrines of demons. (1Timothy 4:1) Signs which demonstrate we are certainly in those days and are increasing day by day. The numbers of sexual scandals which are being exposed in the lives of popular high-profile leaders, has revealed more live a double life. One life is their ministry face and reputation where they are pretending to live holy for the Lord, the other their private life of sexual immorality. The hypocrisy of leaders being excused from their immoral practices by those who are part of their ministry teams is unconscionable.

Why are Christians looking the other way when their ministry leaders are committing blatant hypocrisy, and exploiting the Church with pretense? One might be alarmed by Scriptural warnings which say evil men and imposters will wax worse and worse deceiving and being deceived. Leaders who creep into silly women's homes who can be exploited, who are laden down with many sins. Christian leaders with Church members engaging in sexual immorality. The moral standard among Christians is in crisis, as many who profess faith in Christ simply now live together outside of marriage. Many teen age Church going Christians have no conviction that sex outside of marriage is even wrong. With so many caught into deception, correcting corruption in the lives of leaders seems to be fallen away. For years, an immoral leader may be protected by those who are around him until public scandal finally breaks out, so the whole world can mock and ridicule the hypocrisy.

Can the Church so loose its witness of Christ so it actually fosters an antichrist spirit, and prepares the way from the coming Antichrist? It may surprise many Christians who have been taught an optimistic philosophy the Christ will not return for a dirty Bride. However, the Scriptures speak of the complete opposite reality. For in fact even in the first century Church false prophets had already risen spreading their doctrines of demons. The apostle John in his letters exposed these false prophets were actually working by an antichrist spirit. The end result would lead to apostasy, where many Christians would fall away from the faith in denying the Lord. John was given to expose the antichrist spirit in the Church and warn of the coming, man of sin the actual Antichrist in person.

1 John 4:1-3
1 Beloved, believe not every spirit, but try the spirits whether they are of God: because many false prophets are gone out into the world.
2 Hereby know ye the Spirit of God: Every spirit that confesseth that Jesus Christ is come in the flesh is of God:
3 And every spirit that confesseth not that Jesus Christ is come in the flesh is not of God: and this is that spirit of antichrist, whereof ye have heard that it should come; and even now already is it in the world.

John was shown a great mystery later in visions of the end days, where the coming Great Tribulation was revealed . John saw Mystery Babylon the Great Mother of Harlots who had joined herself with the kingdom of the Antichrist. John wondered with great amazement at the Great Whore who joined with Antichrist, the apostate Church and Christianity in apostasy. Not only will Lord return at a time when the Church has a dirty Bride, the anti-Christ Church makes way in becoming the Bride of the Antichrist. A Great whorish anti-Christian apostasy which started in the first century and will be finalized throughout the whole world as apostate Christianity.

We live in the days where Christians are departing from Bible morality. Celebrate false prophets who itch ears with the Christian fantasies they heap together and only want to hear. We live in days were sexual predators feed their lusts upon the flock of Jesus Christ. We live in days where the message of the Cross is considered old fashioned and out of touch with modern culture. We live in days where sin is no longer sin, and correction of sin has long ago been eliminated from our pulpits. We live in a day where Christians believe there are many paths to God, and it is wrong to judge another person's religion. We live in the days where the Pope of the Catholic Church is unifying all religions in to one worldwide super religion. We live in days where many Christians have come to believe there is no coming

Antichrist, no Great Falling Away, no coming Great Tribulation, or the world ending in a Great Apocalypse.

The Gospel of our day is a Christianity without the Cross, and God's love accepts every man just as they are. Do the false prophets have a voice in the Church today? The answer is obvious, the spirit of antichrist is at work in the end times Church preparing the way for the coming Antichrist.

For those who have ears to hear and eyes to see the Trumpet must be blown warning the enemy is inside the household of the faith.

2 Timothy 3:6-13
6 For of this sort are they which creep into houses, and lead captive silly women laden with sins, led away with divers' lusts,
7 Ever learning, and never able to come to the knowledge of the truth.
8 Now as Jannes and Jambres withstood Moses, so do these also resist the truth: men of corrupt minds, reprobate concerning the faith.
9 But they shall proceed no further: for their folly shall be manifest unto all men, as theirs also was.
10 But thou hast fully known my doctrine, manner of life, purpose, faith, longsuffering, charity, patience,
11 Persecutions, afflictions, which came unto me at Antioch, at Iconium, at Lystra; what persecutions I endured: but out of them all the Lord delivered me.

12 Yea, and all that will live godly in Christ Jesus shall suffer persecution.

13 But evil men and seducers shall wax worse and worse, deceiving, and being deceived.

Revelation 17:1-5

1 And there came one of the seven angels which had the seven vials, and talked with me, saying unto me, Come hither; I will shew unto thee the judgment of the great whore that sitteth upon many waters:

2 With whom the kings of the earth have committed fornication, and the inhabitants of the earth have been made drunk with the wine of her fornication.

3 So he carried me away in the spirit into the wilderness: and I saw a woman sit upon a scarlet-coloured beast, full of names of blasphemy, having seven heads and ten horns.

4 And the woman was arrayed in purple and scarlet colour, and decked with gold and precious stone sand pearls, having a golden cup in her hand full of abominations and filthiness of her fornication:

5 And upon her forehead was a name written, MYSTERY, BABYLON THE GREAT, THE MOTHEROF HARLOTS AND ABOMINATIONS OF THE EARTH.

Chapter Nine
Testing the Spirits

Not Listening To God

Why is it in the Book of Revelation after judging each of the 7 Churches Jesus Christ ends His message with these words: "He that hath an ear, let him hear what the Spirit saith unto the churches." It is like Christ knows even though I Am saying these things many in the Church "don't have ears to hear it." What is the problem then? Christians are not always willing to hear what God "really has to say." I want to suggest with all the prophetic people running around in the Charismatic Movement telling everyone else how to hear God, and all these powerful heavenly encounters, the truth is we have a problem just listening to God tell us things we do not want to hear. Have you ever heard anyone say, I just do not want to hear that, or do not say that to me anymore? The truth is when a person does not agree with you, they will sometimes close their ears to what you are saying. Simply put they have made up their own minds to what they think and feeling and are unwilling to hear what you have to say.

The real problem in the modern prophetic Movement is the prophets are acting like Christians really want to hear what God is saying to them. In Scriptures, what God had to say often was very agitating, brought division, upset the apple cart, made people mad and resentful. As a Christian have you ever really thought about how "unwilling you are to hear God's Word for your life." After all, then you would become responsible for the information, and you will be held accountable for your obedience to the Word of God. This is one reason why modern Charismatics think so little of the Written Word of God, and would rather follow personal revelation, personal prophecy. In this way they can say "God told Me, or God showed me," even if what they say God has said goes against the Written Word of God.

Have you ever thought all the prophetic hype about hearing God, is just an escape from "hearing what the Spirit is saying to the Churches?" The amount of false predictive words, prophetic declarations, is just a loud shout of millions of Charismatics saying, "God I am unwilling to really listen to what you have to say." It is a cover up for closing your heart to God, and rebellion by suppressing the voice of truth. You will often see this fall from grace in high visibility men who are declared prophets. They fall into immorality, some believe they are Elijah, others great end time reformers like Martin Luther. Why do men who speak to angels fall from such great heights of super spirituality?

The truth is speaking to angels, having visions, or translations into heaven, do not supersede the simple voice of God, as written in the Bible. Here is a stunning fact, Christians who are submitted to the Written Word of God are far more in touch with what the Holy Spirit is saying, than prophets who market heavenly visions and angelic encounters. Do you not know your body is the Temple of the Holy Spirit, and the Holy Spirit indwells you? Holy Spirit is your guide and teacher, Holy Spirit will bring to your remembrance the things Jesus Christ has taught and spoken. You do not need a prophetic experience, a heavenly encounter, to hear God. No man needs to teach you to hear God as you have an anointing from God, Holy Spirit and He teaches you all things.

I would say in all the super spirituality of the Prophetic Movement is a great deal of pride and rebellion to God. The number of false predictions, lying visions, hype, and marketing and exploitation of the Church, doctrines of demons, heresy, and New Age witchcraft is absolute proof many Charismatics are really unwilling to hear what the Spirit is saying to the Churches. Here is a simple word of God, something the Lord Jesus Christ is really saying: "As many as I love, I rebuke and chasten: be zealous therefore, and repent. Behold, I stand at the door, and knock: if any man hear my voice, and open the door, I will come into him, and will sup with him, and he with me. To him that overcometh will I grant to sit with me in my throne, even as I also overcame, and am set down with my Father in his throne. He that hath an ear, let him hear what the Spirit saith unto the churches." (Revelation 3:19-22)

Why Create A False Prophetic Narrative

It has become popular for Charismatic Christians to follow a man who is proclaimed as a prophet or apostle because they proclaim personal revelations from God. Most of these self-proclaimed prophets are constantly trying to predict the future. It has become more like fortune tellers who want to tell the future they say has come to them by supernatural revelation. One must ask, why are so many people wanting to know the future, and why are so many Christians caught up into supposed predictive words of prophecy? The answer is related to mans limited capacity, as God has omniscience man does not. In the Christian life God requires us to walk by faith taking God at His Word, even when circumstances are in contradiction to what God has spoken.

When man attempts to know the future apart from what God has already said what would happen according to what the Scriptures say, Man falls into forbidden practices. Instead of walking with God by faith, having to trust by faith what is unseen, an attempt is made to know the future when God has not revealed it. Can God show particular future events? Absolutely yes. However, those times always reveal some purpose which has already been declared by the Written Word of God. Do you understand the Holy Spirit wants to magnify Jesus Christ, and any revelation which exalts a man, or diminishes the Word of God is not the Holy Spirit?

So many who are prophetic have opened themselves up wanting to see what God does not want them to know. Yet, they persist in seeking for the unknown, and finally they find it but not by God. Of course, Satan wants to capture men into a false future and is very active in giving dreams, visions, and angelic encounters which show future events. Why create a false future? A man will follow a path according to their beliefs and understanding. When men refuse the council of Scriptures, the temptation comes to twist the Word of God making say something which God has not said. Today in the Charismatic Movement many so called prophets and apostles have abandoned the doctrine of the Book of Revelation, by teaching all judgments have already passed. To them the doctrine of future end time judgments before the Second Coming of the Lord is not what they want to hear or believe. Instead, they must create a new narrative which teaches the Church makes the world Christian. They have denied the decrease of this age, and create a new philosophy of a better world, a better man.

It is much like the false scenario of fake news. Those who hold platforms of broadcasting do not agree with this Presidency, so they seek to manipulate public opinion by denying the facts and creating their own made-up narrative. It is a constant barrage of misinformation, partial truths, and outright lies which are treated as factual. The Charismatic Prophetic has become very similar. Prophets who do not like how the Bible teaches the future ending of a coming Great Tribulation. So, they claim "special revelation," by constant predictions of the "next big thing from God," creating a false narrative which matches their end time worldwide Church take over philosophy.

Why create such blatant lies and failed predictions? It is simple, not one fact from the Word of God supports this narrative, and not one city or nation has ever become the Kingdom of Heaven on earth for almost 2000 years. Instead of facts, manipulation of people's perception is utilized. What better way to deceive the ignorant and gullible than to create a false future by saying God gave me a vision. Today we live in a world were men like to play God by making up a false story, so as to lead people's minds into a belief which has already made for them. A false scenario because the truth needs to be covered up by all these lies.

The modern Charismatic Prophetic ministry is the land of make believe for all those who refuse the council of God already declared by the Scriptures. One false scenario of failed prophecy after the next false prophetic prediction. Where are the prophets who will teach the full council of God without compromise? Where are the prophets who are willing to warn the masses to flee from the coming wrath of God?

Understanding Godly Rebuke

The Bible is clear when leaders sin, they are to be openly rebuked so all the Church may learn to fear the

Lord. The basis of a Godly rebuke in the Greek is "elegcho," meaning to convict, to convince, to tell a fault. It is an open exposure of sin, of error, of deception with a public confrontation. A Biblical rebuke is not some Christian leader making an apology or posturing before rebuking or correcting so the individual in sin will not feel offended. The cost of rebuking a fellow elder or believer is to defend the integrity of the faith. One the part of the sinful elders, their hypocrisy and guilt are exposed for all to see without apology.

Why a rebuke? It demonstrates the seriousness of the matter. Not only before God but serves as a warning of future judgment at the Second Coming of Jesus Christ. A rebuke has more intensity that a general correction. It has the passion of the Lord, with mercy and grace, yet with Godly anger and confrontation. It is an act of love done in a discipline, which will bring reproach upon anyone who refuses to hear and repent.

What if you are an elder, and your friend is the one whom you must rebuke. Should you in any manner give a break, or lessen the rebuke on the basis of friendship? The Bible is clear correction based upon rebuke is done without respect of persons. As Gods truth is the same measure for all, show no partiality in judgment which would be corruption in justice. The Bible is clear elders who are in sin are to be rebuked openly that all may fear.

1 Timothy 5
20 Them that
sin rebuke before all, that others also may fear.
21 I charge thee before God, and the
Lord Jesus Christ, and the elect angels, that thou
observe these things without preferring one before
another, doing nothing by partiality.
22 Lay hands suddenly on no man, neither be partaker
of other men's sins: keep thyself pure.
23 Drink no longer water, but use a
little wine for thy stomach's sake and thine often infirmi
ties.
24 Some men's sins are open beforehand, going
before to judgment; and some men they follow after.
25 Likewise also the good works of some are manifest
beforehand; and they that are otherwise cannot be hid.
Now let us apply a Godly rebuke to the sin of the
prophets in the Charismatic Movement. Years of false
prophecy has come to a head, in open shame and
hypocrisy. Apologies have been made from some who
are called prophets, and others continue to hold on to
their deception. Many of their ministry friends are to
who they have made themselves accountable. Of
course, they have said they are forgiven, and want to
move on. What is the problem? No public rebuke,
consequences in discipline, and correction. The world
has gone into mocking the failed prophetic predictions,
and Christians are faltering in their faith. The only
recourse for the plague of sin to stop is open rebuke,
that all may fear. Without open rebuke, the sin is

whitewashed, and the Church is considered hypocritical, as we bear false witness and testimony.

Now let us see the instruction from the Book of Titus, where the prophets had given false testimony. Titus was instructing the elders to hold fast to sound doctrine, stopping those who were subverting the truth inside house Churches. One of their own prophets spoke wrongly effecting the opinion of the whole Church. Titus warned the elders to rebuke the prophets sharply for misguiding the Church. The outcome is the prophets who were in deception by sharp rebuke might recovery themselves, being sound in the faith.

What happens when modern prophets are not sharply rebuked? The confrontation of sin and the call to repentance is not complete. When a fallen prophet seeks to justify their actions in a shallow repentance, which has no real consequences. Here is something sad but has been happening with prophets when being confronted with their false witness in the name of the Lord. They have accused those who are confronting them with not being loving and bringing division to the body of Christ. How dangerous for a prophet who has been in error, to accuse those who are confronting of being unloving. Also, the prophets have said they are being persecuted after confessing their error. The persecution would be of a different nature if the Church would fulfill the command to rebuke openly elders in sin.

Just how sharp can a Godly rebuke actually be? Just look at the rebuke Jesus gave the Pharisees for their corruption of doctrine, and hypocrisy in sin. Was Jesus Christ being unloving by calling the Pharisees a brood of vipers, and children of Hell?

Why won't many ministry leaders risk a Godly rebuke? They will lose friendships, ministry partners, and ministry platforms. As the prophet or apostle which they must rebuke has been idolized by his own Movement.

Titus 1:9-16
9 Holding fast the faithful word as he hath been taught, that he may be able by sound doctrine both to exhort and to convince the gainsayers.
10 For there are many unruly and vain talkers and deceivers, specially they of the circumcision:
11 Whose mouths must be stopped, who subvert whole houses, teaching things which they ought not, for filthy lucre's sake.
12 One of themselves, even a prophet of their own, said, The Cretians are alway liars, evil beasts, slow bellies.
13 This witness is true. Wherefore rebuke them sharply, that they may be sound in the faith;
14 Not giving heed to Jewish fables, and commandments of men, that turn from the truth.

15 Unto the pure all things are pure: but unto them that are

defiled and unbelieving is nothing pure; but even their mind and conscience is defiled.

16 They profess that they know God; but in works they deny him, being abominable, and disobedient, and unto every good work reprobate.

Matthew 23:11-33

11 But he that is greatest among you shall be your servant.

12 And whosoever shall exalt himself shall be abased; and he that shall humble himself shall be exalted.

13 But woe unto you, scribes and Pharisees, hypocrites! for ye shut up the kingdom of heaven against men: for ye neither go in yourselves, neither suffer ye them that are entering to go in.

14 Woe unto you, scribes and Pharisees, hypocrites! for ye devour widows' houses, and for a pretence make long prayer: therefore ye shall receive the greater damnation.

15 Woe unto you, scribes and Pharisees, hypocrites! for ye compass sea and land to make one proselyte, and when he is made, ye make him twofold more the child of hell than yourselves.

16 Woe unto you, ye blind guides, which
say, Whosoever shall swear by the temple, it
is nothing; but whosoever shall swear by the gold of the
temple, he is a debtor!
17 Ye fools and blind: for whether is greater, the
gold, or the temple that sanctifieth the gold?
18 And, Whosoever shall swear by the altar, it
is nothing; but whosoever sweareth by the gift that is
upon it, he is guilty.
19 Ye fools and blind: for whether is greater, the
gift, or the altar that sanctifieth the gift?
20 Whoso therefore shall swear by the
altar, sweareth by it, and by all things thereon.
21 And whoso shall swear by the
temple, sweareth by it, and by him that
dwelleth therein.
22 And he that shall swear by heaven, sweareth by the
throne of God, and by him that sitteth thereon.
23 Woe unto
you, scribes and Pharisees, hypocrites! for ye pay
tithe of mint and anise and cummin, and have
omitted the weightier matters of the
law, judgment, mercy, and faith: these ought ye to have
done, and not to leave the other undone.
24 Ye blind guides, which strain at a gnat, and swallow a
camel.
25 Woe unto
you, scribes and Pharisees, hypocrites! for ye make
clean the outside of the cup and of the
platter, but within they are full of extortion and excess.

26 Thou blind Pharisee, cleanse first that which
is within the cup and platter, that the outside of them
may be clean also.
27 Woe unto
you, scribes and Pharisees, hypocrites! for ye are like
unto whited sepulchres, whichindeed appear beautiful o
utward, but are within full of dead men's bones, and of
all uncleanness.
28 Even so ye also outwardly appear righteous unto
men, but within ye are full of hypocrisy and iniquity.
29 Woe unto
you, scribes and Pharisees, hypocrites! because ye
build the tombs of the prophets, and garnish the
sepulchres of the righteous,
30 And say, If we had been in the
days of our fathers, we would not have
been partakers with them in the blood of the prophets.
31 Wherefore ye be witnesses unto yourselves, that ye
are the children of them which killed the prophets.
32 Fill ye up then the measure of your fathers.
33 Ye serpents, ye generation of vipers, how can ye
escape the damnation of hell?

When Prophets Seduce the Immature

We have an interesting thing going on in America where
peoples who are guilty of creating a problem are now
attempting to fix the situation which they have caused.
Why is this interesting, because these same peoples
refuse to see the depth of the problem in their own

lives. In this way the Bible exhortation of taking the log out of your own eye first before attempting to take a sliver out of another is truly applicable. The deepest sense of hypocrisy is on display with guilty leaders in government inside and outside the Church.

Inside the Church the Charismatic Movement is attempting to "fix" a problem of false prophets and false prophecy which they have created for decades. I find it interesting many of the greatest offenders, who have given false predictions for years are now front and center "confronting the deception." Here is what alarming about this level of hypocrisy. Right now, leaders who are guilty themselves are pointing to the guidelines of the Scriptures and are teaching we need to abide by Christ centrality, and the doctrines of Christ. We are to avoid extremes in revelations, and subjective and personal experiences above the written Word of God. Yet, for years the Church has confronted them about this very thing in their own ministries. During that time, they refused correction using such statements as "touch not Gods anointed," or "listen to the prophets and you will prosper." These hypocritical leaders had placed themselves above correction, and now are acting all holy about their deception.

The Bible warns about corrupt leaders using the powers of seduction to draw away the ignorant and immature from Jesus Christ and unto themselves. So much has been marketed about God restoring modern day apostles and prophets according to Ephesians 4. A declaration of proper Church government by a five-fold ministry. However, the apostle and prophet are to guard the flock against exploitation and deception, and not be guilty of creating it. Apostles and prophets who used their ministry platforms to seduce the immature, who have tossed about the immature, and carried them into strange places outside of the safety of Jesus Christ. These same apostles and prophets who are now saying it is dangerous to follow prophecy and give up your discernment to another person.

Why is this hypocrisy happening? Because the continue themselves to use deception, and cunning craftiness so as not to be exposed completely. Here is a great danger! Today they act like they are correcting the false prophetic and tomorrow they are back to their old ways. How can a supposed prophetess go on record confronting false prophetic, then the next days she teaches on "portals into heaven," or living on fasting by sunlight and air only." Can you see the depth of hypocrisy! They cannot see the depth of their own corrupted nature and want to escape their own exposure and hypocrisy, by play acting they are correcting false prophets when they continue to be one! The apostolic and prophetic Movement is in the depth of this hypocrisy. None who are exposed are laying down their ministries which has brought great seduction and division. A question needs to be addressed; how guilty are they for years in deceiving the

Church, and in deep need of repentance? They have been using a cloak of covetousness to profit from the Church. They have not been willing to renounce their hidden things of dishonesty and are caught up in play acting innocence. Are they practicing cunning craftiness and are guilty of handling the Word of God deceitfully? Are they hiding their guilt behind hypocrisy, and in exposing the corruption still are protecting their lies? Paly acting today, but tomorrow will continue to deceive and seduce the Church once again.

The only true way of escape for those who have lost themselves to this level of Satanic deception is to truly see how they are devouring the flock of innocent, ignorant, immature sheep. They are in gross danger before the Lord and must be willing to lay down their ministries. However, to give up the idol of self is more than most will be willing to stop worshipping.

Ephesians 4:14-15
14 That we henceforth be no more children, tossed to and fro, and carried about with every wind of doctrine, by the sleight of men, and cunning craftiness, whereby they lie in wait to deceive;
15 But speaking the truth in love, may grow up into him in all things, which is the head, even Christ:

2 Corinthians 4:2
2 But have renounced the hidden things of dishonesty, not walking in craftiness, nor handling the

word of God deceitfully; but by manifestation of the truth commending ourselves to every man's conscience in the sight of God.

Chapter Ten
Prophets Who Do not Preach the Cross

I have come from inside the Prophetic Charismatic Movement for the last 30 plus years. I have known in some degree many persons of Charismatic prophets who are a part of leading the Movement. The theological errors and non-Biblical practices which have occurred over the last twenty years inside the Movement has led to my departure, and protest against what has been developing. Also, I have seen a growing trend of many other Charismatics who can no longer abide in the deception which has been rapidly progressing. The Prophet Charismatic Movement is beset with many issues which are mainly ignored or even covered up inside the Movement. Rarely will any leader inside the Movement risk any public correction as this is likely to go unheeded and will result in censure of the man who stands by the confrontation. I have seen up to this point many thousands of Christians speaking out against the false doctrines, the thousands of false prophetic predictions, and New Age practices. However, an elitist mentality presides inside the Charismatic Prophetic Movement which nullifies any real consideration they might be deceived or in error.

What I say, I have said out of conviction knowing I also have played a part in the past with many of the same beliefs and practices. So, you might consider my concern an awakening, and a return to the centrality of Jesus Christ. What can be said of the major error which has become normalized inside the Prophetic Movement? The error is to place prophetic words into a place of influence which has pushed them out of the bounds of Biblical Christianity. What does the fruit of thousands of prophetic predictions look like today? A whole lot of false prophecy, and a whole lot of New Age practices. Of course, even though practices like Tarot card reading, and fortune telling, and astral travel all have been normalized inside the Movement, no real recognition of New Age psychic practices are admitted. Instead, a belief of connecting people with supernatural experiences is the high-water mark and belief. Why? Charismatic prophetic teaches Christians to recover the New Age as it has been stolen from the Church. In this way supernatural experiences done by Christians are believed to be the Kingdom of Heaven come to earth by hosting the presence of God. No thought is given to any kind of evil spirit deception, as Charismatics are taught their integrity keeps them from being deceived.

How is all this counterfeit prophetic ministry played out? The height of ministry comes from a personal encounter, a heavenly experience, a vision, a dream, a word of prophecy from God. The more a prophet can validate his experience with supernatural events like an angel came, or Jesus appeared and spoke with me, or I went to heaven and spoke with a dead prophet like Elijah the more weight of credibility is given to the prophetic word. All the time among the apostles and prophets of the Movement you will hear of the next great encounter, vision, or angelic encounter as they seem to come in a great deluge these days. However, when you test many of these experiences, they ring hollow are more sensational and meant to excite an emotional response of "wow" bringing much attention to the prophet who revealed the great encounter. It is odd how little prophetic words need to match up with the Bible, as that would make prophetic words just common and nothing that unusual. It is like the dueling prophets have arisen, and each prophetic experience must exceed what has been before.

What is the deception? In the Prophetic Movement Charismatics are bored with doctrinal teaching and preaching. Instead of preaching Jesus Christ and Him crucified, growing in the doctrines of faith, sensationalism, mysticism, and religious fervor are taught to be the work of the Holy Spirit. In a Prophetic Meeting you will constantly hear of subjective revelation and experiences related to it. Where is the preaching and teaching of Jesus Christ so the Holy Spirit might convict and lead, and teach, and speak into the lives by the written Word of God. No, this is not what happens. Events which are spiritual in appearance, and subjective revelations replace the Word of God. New light of personal revelation has become the manner of preaching and teaching. The danger is so great subjective revelation is put up as final authority over the written word of God as demonstrated by the numbers of false prophecies which go uncorrected. Of course, those leaders inside the Movement insist their preaching and practice is orthodox related to the Cross and the person of Jesus Christ. Instead, you will see spirit emphasis all the time over the preaching of the person Jesus Christ. It is spirit, it is subjective, it is always the voice, what God is saying. It places what is called Holy Spirit ahead of Jesus Christ. While the true work of the Holy Spirit Jesus Christ is magnified not spirit.

If you do not think personal subjective revelation has taken over the Prophetic Movement, consider the rewriting of the Bible inside the Movement. The Passion Translation came about by subjective vision in which Jesus told the false prophet to rewrite the Bible. In accordance with this deception, the false Jesus revealed John chapter 22 which has not yet been written will be given to the end time Charismatic Worldwide World Super Church. No one inside the Movement cried foul and deception, as they all shouted for glory in embracing this lying vision. Having fully endorsed the rewriting of thousands of Scriptures in the Passion Translation Charismatic Bible. It is proof positive each one believes subjective new light on Scriptures is the final authority and word. That is why the Cross of Jesus Christ is almost never preached inside the Prophetic Movement.

Satan's False Gospel

Did you know one of the main tactics in spiritual warfare is Satan's attempt to get you to accept his imitation counterfeit as the authentic? The great imitation of God is going on today all over the world, and even in the Church. It is not what looks blatantly false or evil, it is what is evil hidden by the appearance of good, truthful, and even beautiful. Satan has the false Trinity, the False Godhead, where the False Messiah is soon to appear, the Son of Perdition, the Antichrist. The Great Dragon himself seeks worship as God and sows the false prophets and messengers who proclaim the false Gospel. Did you know Satan has invaded the Church throughout the world by sowing another Jesus, and a false Gospel which leads the masses away from true worship of Jesus Christ?

Did you know the true Gospel appears to be foolish to the minds of men who are darkened in their understanding? The preaching of the Cross is an offense to the perishing, it appears as a foolish message. Did you also know the preaching of the False Gospel is very popular and draws the masses by the multiple millions into a false light and counterfeit salvation? Hundreds of millions of souls have been drawn into counterfeit religions, and religious organizations trapped and enslaved by the false Gospel. Why are so many drawn into the counterfeit if it were just a neutral situation. However, the Prince of the Power of the Air has designed the False Gospel as an imitation so as to keep men under the deception they serve God, so as not to expose Satan is right in their midst. How many are willing to give their lives to the Prince of Darkness under the delusion their false Gospel is Gods true message. Men and women who are led down the prime rose path only to wake up in the Fires of Hell seduced by the lies of a False Gospel. Satan works his tireless temptation to suppress the authentic Gospel of Jesus Christ with great swelling words of vanity, which deny the one and only true God and Great King, Jesus Christ. Why do you reject the message of the Cross? The answer is simple, you have accepted a counterfeit system of false beliefs which have originated from the Kingdom of Darkness.

The deception of the false Gospel runs deep in other religions, but what of the organized Church? Satan's master ploy is to sow the seeds of a corrupted Gospel right among the wheat, the Sons of God. Did you know the most popular Gospel inside the modern organized Church is the one which has minimized the Cross, and exalted man's ideas and philosophy in its place? Did you know the Bible predicts in the last days the false Gospel will be the message Christians run after? In fact, they will shut their ears to the message of the Cross refusing to submit their lives to Jesus Christ and will turn to Christian fables. The Church will seek after men who are willing to preach the false Gospel, Christian Fables, so as to have the ears itched by only being told what they want to hear. The problem will be so chronic they will heap for themselves the false prophets, the false apostles, the false teachers who carry another Gospel by another spirit, which leads to another Jesus which is carried about by doctrines of demons and evil spirits.

We are already deep in those days! What is one of the greatest dangers of modern Christianity? To follow a man, a women who preaches an imitation Gospel which seduces the Church to follow an imitation Satanic Jesus. Will Christians know they are being deceived? Yes and no. Many will warn of the false apostles and false prophets which are in the pulpits. Many will use the Scriptures to expose the False Gospel and False Messengers. However, the seduction has come with Christians to ignore the Scriptures or even undermine the Scriptures through unbelief. In short, they will not take the Bible as their final authority and will not submit to the Scriptures in the literal teaching.
As a Christian you can suppress the truth by manipulating the Scriptures to say something the original text does not say. The False Gospel is simply a manipulation of the Scriptures by putting a private interoperation of man's ideas and philosophy in its place. Satan is deep into the Church which has allowed men of fame and fortune to undermine the Gospel. Did

know men who call themselves apostles and prophets have heartedly approved of the rewriting of Scriptures to manufacture an imitation Bible with their philosophical beliefs rewritten and infused into the Scriptures. Watch out for any Christian Movement that needs to rewrite the Bible to fit their narrative, and endorse they alone have the proper understanding of Scriptures. As these has already happened in the Charismatic Movement, one can only question is the Great Apostasy from the faith well underway. Lead by Satan's end time False Gospel?

2 Timothy 4:1-5
1 I charge thee therefore before God, and the Lord Jesus Christ, who shall judge the quick and the dead at his appearing and his kingdom;
2 Preach the word; be instant in season, out of season; reprove, rebuke, exhort with all longsuffering and doctrine.
3 For the time will come when they will not endure sound doctrine; but after their own lusts shall they heap to themselves teachers, having itching ears;
4 And they shall turn away their ears from the truth, and shall be turned unto fables.
5 But watch thou in all things, endure afflictions, do the work of an evangelist, make full proof of thy ministry

Prophecy or Gospel In Times of Catastrophic Events

Should the Church be active in making predictions by prophecy about the effects of the Coronavirus? All most all Coronavirus prophecy comes from Charismatic Preterists who always put a positive spin on their predictions. One famous Charismatic prophet went on record before the Coronavirus was declared to be pandemic, the virus would stop and soon disappear. After which the same prophet said millions would not die from the virus plague. Of course, anyone who can think for themselves does not need a prophet to tell us millions will not die, as even influenzas are more deadly than the Coronavirus. The medical industry has put the mortality rate at 1 to 2%, and usually related to the elderly with preexistent conditions. In no way do I consider many of the prophetic predictions as actual words of prophecy from God. Instead, these are doctrinal beliefs being presented in a super spiritual way of putting out Preterists doctrinal beliefs. They are blend of Charismatic Preterist doctrine of worldwide Church take over and blended with the practice of giving predictions related to social and cultural events of interest.

Why would Charismatic prophecy be constantly employed as a means to say God is speaking? What is more Biblically proper? The preaching of the Gospel connecting the masses to Gods redemptive plan of eternal redemption. Are the prophets being tempted to keep a platform alluring an audience by drawing people unto themselves as one who has God's message. Why is the seduction of drawing men to a Charismatic prophet a complete falsehood? The Gospel does not lead men to a prophet or a prophetic word, instead directs men to the Cross of Jesus Christ. Throughout the 2000 years of Church history the world has battled epidemics, and world wars, and great catastrophic events but the Gospel of eternal salvation has never changed. As the Gospel of salvation transcends the temporal events of this present evil age and deals with a man's eternal state. The message of the Church is not prophecy or predictive prophecy, as this gift of the Holy Spirit will pass away. However, the doctrines of Jesus Christ are the eternal Word of God and are infallible and immutable.

Is God speaking a clear word concerning the nations, and the masses, and what is coming upon the earth? Yes, thousands of years ago Jesus Christ spoke the more sure word of prophecy which dictated the events of the last days. Earthquakes, famines, and plagues are just a part which will led to the final end time judgments called the Great Tribulation. Should I use prophecy to manipulate people into my doctrinal beliefs, so people would say; "you are a real prophet?" If I am a Charismatic Preterist and do not believe in end time judgments, should I use predictive prophecy to say; "God showed me these are not judgments from God?" You are manipulating people using the name of God, by saying "God showed me, or God told me." Instead of preaching and declaring your doctrinal beliefs which are your own personal convictions and not God's revelations or Holy Spirit words of prophecy.

For these very reasons, the Charismatic Movement has fallen to false prophecy and failed predictive words. The facts are Charismatics make false predictions by the dozens or the hundreds, and then claim words which are somewhat related to circumstances as evidence. Let us get this right, the failure of predictions out numbers anything which could be considered a true prediction 1000 to 1. If you are a Charismatic Prophet, are you as willing to show all the failed false prophecy you have given, as compared to an occasional word which would be considered a true prediction? Who would be willing to follow a man or woman that fails most of the times in a prediction, or would consider them as God's prophet who gives true words from God? Those outside the Preterist Charismatic Prophetic Movement record your false predictions all the time and declare your failed prophecies as evidence you are a false prophet. Are they wrong to expose this hypocrisy, and make judgments of false ministries?

On the other hand, a man who preaches the Gospel will always be effective , as the Gospel itself is the power of God unto salvation. The Gospel is self-sufficient needing no props, no prophecy, no manifestations of any kind to authenticate its eternal salvation. Even if a man were never to hear a prophetic word, but heard the Gospel, the more sure word of prophecy is included as the doctrines of Jesus Christ in the Gospel. For Christ's predictions of the Second Coming are an unfailing confirmation of the Gospel of Salvation. Even if a man were never to see or experience a physical healing, the Gospel by itself has all the power necessary to save a man from eternal damnation and give them a furtive resurrection into an immortal body.

The Gospel of our salvation is vastly superior to any contemporary prophetic word. Why then is prophecy given in the midst of crisis, and not the Gospel? Is this not an ultimate deception, and proof of doctrines of demons and seducing spirits inside the Church?

2 Timothy 4:1-8
1 I charge thee therefore before God, and the Lord Jesus Christ, who shall judge the quick and the dead at his appearing and his kingdom.
2 Preach the word; be instant in season, out of season; reprove, rebuke, exhort with all longsuffering and doctrine.
3 For the time will come when they will not endure sound doctrine; but after their own lusts shall they heap to themselves teachers, having itching ears.
4 And they shall turn away their ears from the truth and shall be turned unto fables.
5 But watch thou in all things, endure afflictions, do the work of an evangelist, make full proof of thy ministry.
6 For I am now ready to be offered, and the time of my departure is at hand.

7 I have fought a good fight, I have finished my course, I have kept the faith:

8 Henceforth there is laid up for me a crown of righteousness, which the Lord, the righteous judge, shall give me at that day: and not to me only, but unto all of them also that love his appearing.

5 Reasons Why the Church Needs To Preach the Second Coming

1) This Age and World Is Passing Away
2) The Time Is Short
3) Warning To Flee Gods Coming Wrath
4) All Mankind Will Be Resurrected From the Dead
5) God Will Judge Every Man According To Their Works

1. As compared to an eternity this present age and world has a very limited expiration date. Christians are on a journey through this age, it is not our home. We are moving towards the Coming age, the Kingdom age, and the resurrection of the righteous dead. The Bible describes this age as corrupted by sin and death, and the days are evil. We are commanded to redeem the time, as in comparison to an eternity in the next age, our life here is like a vapor of smoke. Here today gone tomorrow. Trying to make this present evil age your home is like trying to mix oil with water, or light and

darkness. Instead, we are to expose the unfruitful deeds of darkness, and not be partakers with them.

2. Why did the first century Church believe the Second Coming of Jesus Christ would be soon. Was it not the result of the great suffering and martyrdom by Cesar Nero and Rome? Could this for the first century Church be the Great Tribulation and Antichrist, which Jesus Christ said would happen before His return. Paul cleared up the matter in his writings, also then the Lord gave the Apostle John the Book of Revelation In 95 to 98 AD. It has been about two thousand years since, and the time grows very short. The conditions which were predicted by Jesus Christ have become very present in our days. Especially when Israel was made a nation once again in 1948 after thousands of years of being trampled by the Gentile nations. The time has grown very short, and Christians are commanded to watch and pray for the Second Coming.

3. The Bible clearly teaches right before the Second Coming of Jesus Christ is the world's greatest Tribulation every given. If you want to stick your head in the sand along with the false teaching of Charismatic Preterist you have that right to

choose deception. They teach the Book of Revelation has already been 90% completed. All the wrath of God was already poured out in the first century Church. So instead of warning the world to flee from the wrath to come, the Preterists teach a coming Golden Age. The Charismatic Preterists are building a whitewashed wall of worldwide Church take over. A false Gospel called the 7 Mountain Gospel, which teach the Church will cleanse the 7 pillars of culture making the world Christian, "before Jesus Christ can return." They ignore the warnings of Scripture which teach of the Coming Day of the Lord God almighty, a day of great darkness and distress for the whole world.

4. The Second Coming reminds us of connected to the Lord's return are the two resurrections from the dead. Our salvation is not complete until we take off our mortality and are clothed upon by immortality. The doctrine of the Church is the resurrection of the righteous dead, and the Second Coming of Jesus Christ are two interconnected events. There is no such thing as Jesus Coming, and a spiritual glorified state without a bodily resurrection. Only other religions teach a glorified spiritual state without a bodily resurrection. To keep the Church from falling into New Age beliefs or mysticism, the Scriptures teach our glorification is given at the

resurrection from the dead and not before. The Second Resurrection happens 1000 years after the first and is the Great White Throne Judgment Of the unrighteousness dead. Whosoever names are not written in the Book of Life are cast into the Lake of Fire. This is called the Second Death as it occurs after a sinful man is raised from the dead back into his body, to be eternally judged by God in the Lake of Fire.

5. The final judgment for Christians is at the Judgment Seat of Christ, after the Second Coming and the catching up of the Church Into the clouds. God will judge every Christian according to what they have done in their body during their lifetimes. Works are tested by fire, both good and bad, as God is no respecter of persons. For those whom He approves their works, gold, silver, and precious gems, they are given Kingdom age entrance and rewards. For those who buried their talent and would not serve the Lord, they are shut out of the Kingdom age, put Into outer darkness where there will be weeping and gnashing of teeth.

Final thoughts. The Second Coming teaches us to fear the Lord where every man will stand in judgment, to give an account to God. Teaching on the Second Coming gives us faith to look beyond this present evil age, knowing how we live our life now will affect our future eternity.

Revelation 20
1 And I saw an angel come down from heaven, having the key of the bottomless pit and a great chain in his hand.
2 And he laid hold on the dragon, that old serpent, which is the Devil, and Satan, and bound him a thousand years,
3 And cast him into the bottomless pit, and shut him up, and set a seal upon him, that he should deceive the nations no more, till the thousand years should be fulfilled: and after that he must be loosed a little season.
4 And I saw thrones, and they sat upon them, and judgment was given unto them: and I saw the souls of them that were beheaded for the witness of Jesus, and for the word of God, and which had not worshipped the beast, neither his image, neither had received his mark upon their foreheads, or in their hands; and they lived and reigned with Christ a thousand years.
5 But the rest of the dead lived not again until the thousand years were finished. This is the first resurrection.
6 Blessed and holy is he that hath part in the first resurrection: on such the second death hath no power,

but they shall be priests of God and of Christ and shall reign with him a thousand years.

7 And when the thousand years are expired, Satan shall be loosed out of his prison,

8 And shall go out to deceive the nations which are in the four quarters of the earth, Gog, and Magog, to gather them together to battle: the number of whom is as the sand of the sea.

9 And they went up on the breadth of the earth, and compassed the camp of the saints about, and the beloved city: and fire came down from God out of heaven and devoured them.

10 And the devil that deceived them was cast into the lake of fire and brimstone, where the beast and the false prophet are, and shall be tormented day and night for ever and ever.

11 And I saw a great white throne, and him that sat on it, from whose face the earth and the heaven fled away; and there was found no place for them.

12 And I saw the dead, small and great, stand before God; and the books were opened: and another book was opened, which is the book of life: and the dead were judged out of those things which were written in the books, according to their works.

13 And the sea gave up the dead which were in it; and death and hell delivered up the dead which were in them: and they were judged every man according to their works.

14 And death and hell were cast into the lake of fire. This is the second death.

15 And whosoever was not found written in the book of life was cast into the lake of fire.

Charismatic Dominion Theology An Epic Fail
What happened when the Hurricanes came in the last couple of years? Charismatic Dominion Theology attempted to rebuke and decree the storms away. Even when the Charismatics declared they would not bring any damage, not make landing, when the storms passed through, they would declare a measure of victory. Now we have the Coronavirus plague several of the more notable prophets attempted to say it would not be a pandemic and would soon disappear. The prophets did all their predictions by saying God showed me, or God told me, or I had a dream or vision. Of course, all their predictions are an epic failure, as the Pandemic has changed the course of many nations including America. Several of the more notable apostles of Dominion Theology attempted to "make a show of authority" by declaring authority over the Coronavirus plague and then declaring it was finished. Another ridiculous display of false authority born out of Charismatic Dominionism. So many have given a false prophetic declaration, using their hype and manipulation in the name of God which led to a hill of beans. Even notable famous apostles who had declared complete dominion over all sickness and disease had no authority to heal the plague. Instead, the shut down their Charismatic healing conferences fearing the plague would spread increasing the numbers of Christians who would get sick, or even die. All this

pretense and boasting of an authority they do not have, has led to many corrupted and false practices which has damaged the lives of many Christians. Fake dominion authority has failed outside Charismatic conferences where real-life situations overpowered their pretensions.

Will God open the eyes of the millions of Charismatics who follow the false doctrines and practices of Dominion Theology. For years, many false beliefs have invaded the Church by those apostles and prophets who teach this false Gospel. One great example is taught that Christ will not return for a spotted dirty Bride. Dominion preaching falsely teaches Christ will not return until He has purified the whole Church. However, nowhere in Scriptures is the Church going to be purified before the Second Coming. In fact, perilous times are predicted for the last days right inside the Church. Evil men and imposters will wax worse and worse. Many Christians will depart from the faith giving heed to seducing spirits and doctrines of demons. Dominion Theology apostles and prophets attempt to act super spiritual when it comes to the massive amount of sin, and godlessness going onto today in the modern Church. Simply put, the Lord will have a pure spotless bride, but a least half the Church will fail to obtain to that statues. The Parable of the Ten Virgins is just one of the many passages which shows the true condition of the Church at the Second Coming of Jesus Christ.

Another epic fail is to teach and end time super Church. Notice how the Nation is being ripped apart through racial hatred, murder, and violence. Apostles and prophets of Dominion Theology must spin all the demonic darkness and evil which is going on in our day. Notice how Dominion prophets always attempt to say international revival is sure to follow all this hate and evil. Why, because they would have to face the epic failure of the 7 Mountain Gospel which declares the Charismatic Super Church will cleanse the 7 pillars of culture making the nations Christian before Jesus Christ can return. Notice how Charismatics cannot accept the massive amount of human depravity on display. Instead of preaching the Gospel of Salvation confronting mankind's sin and evil nature, they seduce fallen men with smooth speech thinking God is not judging them, and love will change their hatred of God. Sometimes you will never hear a Charismatic Dominionist speak of the need to repent of sin and turn to the Cross of Jesus Christ as the only way to be saved. Instead, they speak prophecies about how great the potential of the man lost in sin will be in the future. Instead of dealing of the man's true spiritual condition today. They think by not offending the person and connecting them with a prophetic presence of God they have brought them into the Kingdom. The Cross and confession of Jesus Christ is nowhere in sight.

Finally, Dominion Theology apostles and prophets are teaching the deification of the Church. All manner of false doctrines are used to support the Charismatic Super Church is filling up with the DNA of God or filling up with the divinity of Christ. One well know multimillionaire super apostle teaches the Church is filling up with the divinity of God, insomuch the body of Christ will be in equal proportions of divinity as the head of the Church Jesus Christ. Another super apostle rewrote the Bible putting in thousands of words or removing them to infuse the Scriptures with Dominion Theology beliefs. The same false apostle teaches the Lord will "return as a reincarnation in the Church," and the book of Revelation has nothing to do with end time judgments of God. The man who says God gave him a vision to rewrite the Bible is a full-fledged heretic. An epic failure of the fantasy and corruption of Charismatic Dominion Theology.

Hebrews 2:1-9

1 Therefore we ought to give the more earnest heed to the things which we have heard, lest at any time we should let them slip.

2 For if the word spoken by angels was stedfast, and every transgression and disobedience received a just recompence of reward.

3 How shall we escape, if we neglect so great salvation, which at the first began to be spoken by the Lord, and was confirmed unto us by them that heard him;

4 God also bearing them witness, both with signs and wonders, and with divers' miracles, and gifts of the Holy Ghost, according to his own will?

5 For unto the angels hath he not put in subjection the world to come, whereof we speak.

6 But one in a certain place testified, saying, What is man, that thou art mindful of him? or the son of man, that thou visitest him?

7 Thou madest him a little lower than the angels; thou crownedst him with glory and honour, and didst set him over the works of thy hands:

8 Thou hast put all things in subjection under his feet. For in that he put all in subjection under him, he left nothing that is not put under him. But now we see not yet all things put under him.

9 But we see Jesus, who was made a little lower than the angels for the suffering of death, crowned with glory and honour; that he by the grace of God should taste death for every man.

Rewriting Scriptures Brings God's Curse

First of all, Christians should never apologize for asking teachers to give an account for what they say, write and teach. This is standard practice from the very beginning of Christian discipleship, as Satan twists the Word of God as one of the Kingdom of Darkness wiles of deception. That is right, Satan is the primary agent in "altering the Word of God," just like at the original temptation in the Garden of Eden where Satan challenged Gods Word. Let us get real, God is intolerant when it comes to disobeying His Word, it is an act of rebellion, and act of treason to the Throne. For if God's Word is not final authority, neither then is God final authority, and if all authority in heaven and earth does not rest with God, He is not God!

Here is something completely silly happening in the Charismatic Prophetic movement. The practice of prophesying a false word. In this way they deny the infallibility of God's written Word. You say how? God has already given the Church the more "sure Word of Prophecy ," written in the Scriptures. The only true infallible prophetic Word are the prophecies of Scriptures, the testimony of Jesus is the Spirit of prophecy. The error comes when Charismatics give prophetic words which are contrary to the doctrines of Christ, false prophecy which speaks against what has already been written.
Let us get real Charismatics have used prophecy to promote their doctrinal beliefs. Anyone who is serious, can see the practice of prophesying "Preterist Philosophy ," the eschatological teachings of Kingdom Now, and worldwide Church take over.

Here comes the danger, the Preterist use false prophecy, wild predictions of worldwide revival, revival angels, and all manner of lying dreams and visions. However, the Charismatic Preterists have gone to the next level, "rewriting Scriptures," to add words, or take away words form thousands of Scriptures to alter the meaning to a Kingdom Now Preterist beliefs. This is not conjecture, it is well documented proven by many different sources. The Charismatic Preterist Bible called the Passion Translation as rewritten by a single Charismatic apostle, is not a faithful Bible translation at all. Said Charismatic apostle has taken the liberty to change thousands of passages, to make the "official Preterist Charismatic Bible." Endorsed by virtually all apostles and prophets of the Prophetic Charismatic Movement."

How was the Passion Translation justified by the Charismatic apostle the author? By a false prophecy and vision of course. Another "God told me, or God showed me," I have a prophetic word, a prophetic encounter from heaven. Here is the big problem, the Scriptures warn "even if an angel from Heaven were to preach (teach, prophecy, or preach) another Gospel, let him be accursed."

Now let us get this right. God said by no means do not change My Word, as God cannot lie, God cannot be corrupted, and God cannot change, His word is "immutable," The warning is God has given His written Word, it is set for all eternity. God will not alter or change it. It is what is, "God has spoken who can but prophecy."

Amos 3:7-8

7 Surely the Lord God will do nothing, but he revealeth his secret unto his servants the prophets.
8 The lion hath roared, who will not fear? the Lord God hath spoken, who can but prophesy?

Did you get that God will never alter His Word? It is the very foundation of His Throne, the foundation of His very person. No man, no angle of God, no vision of Jesus, no fallen angel like Satan, has been given the right, or the authority to rewrite the Scriptures. So, the Charismatic apostle attempted to use "a prophetic vision of Jesus and heaven," a "word of prophecy" to validate his commission from Jesus to "rewrite the Bible." Except this Jesus, could not possibly be the Jesus Christ who is the Lord God of Heaven and Earth. Who then was the Jesus who commissioned this Charismatic apostle? A prophetic vision used to justify the rewriting of Scriptures, and changing their meanings by adding or subtracting thousands of words which were never part of the original passages? A prophetic vision, to rebel against what God has said He would never allow, to alter, to rewrite Scriptures and corrupt the written Word of God? The Jesus of whom commissions the rewriting of Scriptures is no one less than an "angel of light," a fallen dark angel, or even Satan himself. Let us get this right, a fallen dark angel came to the author and gave self-declared apostle a lying vision. A tempting of the Charismatic apostle's pride and elitist beliefs. Just like in the Garden when Satan tempted Adam and Eve to reject God's word.

The whole Prophetic Movement has elevated the false Jesus vision, as God's ordination. Only Satan is the author of the Passion Translation Bible with its corrupted Gospel deception. Which proves how easily angels of light move about freely, in lying dreams, visions, prophecy, and supernatural manifestations inside the Prophetic Movement. What also demonstrates how prophecy has become "doctrine for modern apostles."

Sadly, the author has not inherited God's blessing. Instead has fallen into God's judgment and will inherit God's curse for rewriting the Bible. Though we (apostles) or an angel form heaven preach another Gospel, let him be accursed. I trust Charismatic apostles and prophets can understand the simplicity of this warning. Unfortunately, they have elevated their Kingdom Now/Dominion prophetic philosophy above the authority of God's Word. An abomination in the eyes of God. Should bring the greatest rebuke and censure from every Christian.

Galatians 1:6-12
6 I marvel that ye are so soon removed from him that called you into the grace of Christ unto another gospel:
7 Which is not another; but there be some that trouble you and would pervert the gospel of Christ.

8 But though we, or an angel from heaven, preach any other gospel unto you than that which we have preached unto you, let him be accursed.

9 As we said before, so say I now again, If any man preach any other gospel unto you than that ye have received, let him be accursed.

10 For do I now persuade men, or God? or do I seek to please men? for if I yet pleased men, I should not be the servant of Christ.

11 But I certify you, brethren, that the gospel which was preached of me is not after man.

12 For I neither received it of man, neither was I taught it, but by the revelation of Jesus Christ.

Chapter Eleven
Jesus Christ Warns of False Prophets

Why Jesus Christ Warns of False Prophets

Perhaps the Church has been slow to understand the significance of prophets both true and false. I trust in the modern organized Charismatic Movement self-declared prophets might number in the thousands. A similar phenomena has happened with Charismatic Pastors who overnight declared they were now apostles. Nothing different had really happened, except they might be collecting a few more Churches for their apostolic organizations or speak in a few more conferences. What has become dangerous inside the Movement is to self-declare you are an apostle, or you are a prophet without the genuine fruit or characteristics of that ministry. Let us put it this way Jesus only had twelve apostles, after that only several dozen more are mentioned in the New Testament. The calling of a New Testament apostle, or prophet, does not make one an apostle or prophet. So many want the title without the price which must be paid behind the title.

Why would Jesus warn of false prophets? The problem is in the false prophet's ability to misguide the masses. The issue being how popular are their words to so many, to lead them away from the truth. A false prophet leads the people away from the straight and narrow way unto the broad way of destruction. It seems to be the "right way to so many," however, they follow the seductions of a false prophet away from the Lord. A true prophet, or true apostle will act like a shepherd and see the false prophet and protect the flock. Which leads to the next issue concerning false prophets, their ability to devour the flock.

Simply put, the inner motive of a false ministry is corrupted. False ministries use the Church and exploit it for personal profit and gain. Jesus Christ warned false prophets would come as wolves with sheep's clothing. On the outside the can look convincing, like they are really sent by the Lord. Additionally, many false prophets have some form of the supernatural working in their ministries, so ignorant, or immature Christians will be seduced by displays of power or revelation. In this way false prophets can draw away a crowd of people and bring them under their influences. Look out for self-declared prophets who are using their ministries or giftings to get your money. False prophets motivate you with persuasive words attempting to convince you that you are giving to God when you give to their ministries. Many will come into a Church and rape the Church of all the finances and leave a wake of devastated used and abused sheep. The fruit is really rotten even though the seduction can be very powerful and convincing.

Another thing to watch for is how men react around female members of the Church. A false prophet is at heart an immoral person, who wants to beguile unstable souls. You will often see the prophets using their gifting to drawn women under the influence, so as to exploit them sexually. In this season many false prophets who are big names are being exposed for their multiple sexually immoral relations. Leaving a trail of sexually exploited women in the nations, and Churches where they have been. It seems weekly now the next high-profile personality is exposed for being s sexual predator in the Church. A true prophet will expose the hidden things of darkness and bring them out into the light. A false prophet will hide in hypocrisy play acting as a moral person while exploiting women right under the

Pastors nose. Once a man or woman is taken in adultery while using the name of the Lord, should be immediately removed from ministry, and openly rebuked before all. Any man or woman who refuses this discipline should be marked and removed from the Church.

The apostle Paul disciplined a man who the Church refused to confront in sexual immorality, by delivering the man over to Satan for the destruction of his flesh. A true apostle or prophet is often given a great deal of spiritual authority to bring real correction and discipline to the Church. The apostle Paul knew upon his departure grievous wolves would enter in to devour the flock. What is missing today is the apostolic/prophetic authority to expose the wolves and false prophets to keep the flock from being exploited and devoured. Sadly, many modern Charismatic media platforms actually promote the false prophets and will be held responsible for the destruction false prophets bring.

Matthew 7:13-20

13 Enter ye in at the strait gate: for wide is the gate, and broad is the way, that leadeth to destruction, and many there be which go in thereat:
14 Because strait is the gate, and narrow is the way, which leadeth unto life, and few there be that find it.

15 Beware of false
prophets, which come to you in sheep's clothing, but in
wardly they are ravening wolves.
16 Ye shall know them by their fruits. Do men
gather grapes of thorns, or figs of thistles?
17 Even so every good tree bringeth
forth good fruit; but a corrupt tree bringeth
forth evil fruit.
18 A good tree cannot bring
forth evil fruit, neither can a corrupt tree bring
forth good fruit.
19 Every tree that bringeth not forth good fruit is hewn
down, and cast into the fire.
20 Wherefore by their fruits ye shall know them.

Jesus Christ Warns of False Apostles and Prophets

Maybe the Charismatic Movement is not used to being
exposed with having many false apostles and prophets.
Instead of addressing the issue, justifications will come
from the guilty like "touch not my anointed," or you are
creating division, or you are a heresy hunter. All these
claims are just an avoidance of the issues being
confronted which are false prophecies, false doctrines,
and even heresies. However, is confrontation of the
false true practice of the New Testament?

How can any Christian deny Jesus Christ was the "first
heresy hunter!"

When Jesus Christ judged the 7 Churches in the Book of Revelation, we actually see the confrontation of false apostles, false prophets, and false doctrines, Here is an example from each of the 7 Churches:

Ephesus

The Christians at the Church of Ephesus were commended by the Lord for discerning false apostles, and "not tolerating wicked men."

Revelation 2:2

[2] I know thy works, and thy labour, and thy patience, and how thou canst not bear them which are evil: and thou hast tried them which say they are apostles, and are not, and hast found them liars:

Smyrna

Jesus Christ commended the poverty and difficulty of the Smyrna Christians. Which flies in the face of the world's riches being God's blessing. The Lord highly rewards suffering for righteousness' sake. Though this Church appeared poor and without any real authority, Jesus Christ offers the highest of rewards. These saints would qualify for ruling with Christ in the next age where the power of the Second death would have no rule over them.

Revelation 2:9

⁹ I know thy works, and tribulation, and poverty, (but thou art rich) and I know the blasphemy of them which say they are Jews, and are not, but are the synagogue of Satan.

Pergamos

Christians in Pergamos have the temptation to follow a false prophet of the worse kind, a Balaam like false prophet. This prophet lead the Church into idolatry, and sexual immorality, The severest of warnings is given by Christ, He will come and fight these Christians with the sword out of His mouth. The same judgment Christ uses against the Antichrist, and the False Prophet in the Battle of Armageddon.

Christ also hates the Nicolaitan doctrine which was present in the Church also. Christ hates the bad fruit which comes from false prophets, and false doctrines.

Thyatira

The Christians in Thyatira were following a false prophetess of the worse kind who modeled herself after Queen Jezebel in the Old Testament. Jesus Christ called her work "fornication" and was drawing Christians into idolatry, and sexual immorality. God would judge her with a sick bed, and her children with death. I find it interesting Jesus Christ warns of judgment unto death, when confronting false prophetic ministry. This would go over like a lead balloon in modern prophetic ministry.

Revelation 2:20

20 Notwithstanding I have a few things against thee, because thou sufferest that woman Jezebel, which calleth herself a prophetess, to teach and to seduce my servants to commit fornication, and to eat things sacrificed unto idols. 21 And I gave her space to repent of her fornication; and she repented not. 22 Behold, I will cast her into a bed, and them that commit adultery with her into great tribulation, except they repent of their deeds.23 And I will kill her children with death; and all the churches shall know that I am he which searcheth the reins and hearts: and I will give unto every one of you according to your works.

Sardis

The Christians in Sardis had defiled their garments by their practices. Proves Jesus Christ does judge us by our works. Even though modern Charismatic false teachers and false doctrines teach, all judgment has passed Christians. Only Gods blessings remain. Which makes Jesus Christs judgement of the 7 Churches a complete lie. Do not be deceived all Christians will stand in judgment at the Second Coming of the Lord.

Revelation 3:4

[4] Thou hast a few names even in Sardis which have not defiled their garments; and they shall walk with me in white: for they are worthy. [5] He that overcometh, the same shall be clothed in white raiment; and I will not blot out his name out of the book of life, but I will confess his name before my Father, and before his angels.

Philadelphia

The only Church out of 7 which was commended for not having false doctrines, or false prophets, or false practices. Christ commends them rewarding them with an open door and promise of escape from the coming hour of trial.

Revelation 3:8-10

[8] I know thy works: behold, I have set before thee an open door, and no man can shut it: for thou hast a little strength, and hast kept my word, and hast not denied my name. [9] Behold, I will make them of the synagogue of Satan, which say they are Jews, and are not, but do lie; behold, I will make them to come and worship before thy feet, and to know that I have loved thee.
[10] Because thou hast kept the word of my patience, I also will keep thee from the hour of temptation, which shall come upon all the world, to try them that dwell upon the earth.

Laodicean

A completely deceived Church which cannot see their true state before God. The worlds influence has completely corrupted them before God. Jesus Christ judges them wretched, miserable, poor, blind, and naked. A Church so far removed from following Jesus Christ; He stands at the door knocking outside the Church. They are so compromised before God; He vomits them out of His mouth.

Revelation 3:15-19

[15] I know thy works, that thou art neither cold nor hot: I would thou wert cold or hot.   [16] So then because thou art lukewarm, and neither cold nor hot, I will spue thee out of my mouth.

[17] Because thou sayest, I am rich, and increased with goods, and have need of nothing; and knowest not that thou art wretched, and miserable, and poor, and blind, and naked: [18] I counsel thee to buy of me gold tried in the fire, that thou mayest be rich; and white raiment, that thou mayest be clothed, and that the shame of thy nakedness do not appear; and anoint thine eyes with eyesalve, that thou mayest see.

[19] As many as I love, I rebuke and chasten: be zealous therefore, and repent.

The Apostle Paul Warns of False Prophets

Acts 20:25-30

25 And now, behold, I know that ye all, among whom I
have gone preaching the kingdom of God, shall
see my face no more.
26 Wherefore I take you to
record this day, that I am pure from the blood of
all men.
27 For I have not shunned to declare unto you all the
counsel of God.
28 Take heed therefore unto yourselves, and to all the
flock, over the which the Holy Ghost hath
made you overseers, to feed the church of
God, which he hath purchased with his own blood.
29 For I know this, that after my departing shall
grievous wolves enter in among you, not sparing the
flock.

30 Also of your own
selves shall men arise, speaking perverse things, to draw
away disciples after them.

The Apostle Paul was ordained an apostle by the Holy
Spirit, but first came from those workers who served
the Lord as prophets and teachers. Paul had an
extraordinary revelatory gift which included many open
visions from the Holy Spirit. Paul was able to function
with a great deal of spiritual discernment. So as Paul
was departing for Rome knowing trials and

imprisonment awaited him, Paul gave his final warnings and instructions to the Church elders before his departure.

Paul, said he did not withhold any of the Lords council, and Paul was innocent from the blood of all men. Paul exhorted the elders God had made them overseers, and to be faithful in feeding the Church with proper doctrines in Christ.

Paul by discernment and fore knowledge of the Holy Spirit was able to discern that grievous false prophets would enter into the Church as devouring wolves. Not sparing the flock wolves in sheep's clothing would exploit the Church for their own personal gain. Ironically, Paul saw within the ranks of these elder leaders' men would arise speaking perverse things, to draw away disciples away from the Lord and after them. Now after nearly two thousand years Paul's warning is applicable today as it was back in the first century.

The Apostle John Warns of False Prophets

1 John 4:1-4
Beloved, believe not every spirit, but try the spirits whether they are of God: because many false prophets are gone out into the world.
[2] Hereby know ye the Spirit of God: Every spirit that confesseth that Jesus Christ is come in the flesh is of God
[3] And every spirit that confesseth not that Jesus Christ is

come in the flesh is not of God: and this is that spirit of
antichrist, whereof ye have heard that it should come;
and even now already is it in the world.
⁴ Ye are of God, little children, and have overcome
them: because greater is he that is in you, than he that
is in the world.
⁵ They are of the world: therefore, speak they of the
world, and the world heareth them.
⁶ We are of God: he that knoweth God heareth us; he
that is not of God heareth not us. Hereby know we the
spirit of truth, and the spirit of error.

In the first century Church false prophets had already
invaded the Church bringing in the false Gnostic Gospel.
The apostle John wrote to warn of the false prophets in
his letters to the Church. John lays out instructions to
the saints on how to discern the false prophets in their
midst.

1 John 4:1-4
Beloved, believe not every spirit, but try the spirits
whether they are of God: because many false prophets
are gone out into the world.

The false prophets were functioning by another spirit
other than the Holy Spirit. John said do not just let the
prophets say and do anything they want then to call it
God. Instead, you are to test the spirits of the prophets
to see wither or not they are from God. For the false

prophets have fallen away from the doctrines of Christ and fallen after the spirits of the world.

The apostle John says by testing the spirit of the prophets you can discern by what spirit they minister. The Gnostic prophets denied the incarnation of Jesus Christ and would not say in the person of Jesus Christ God had come in the flesh. Every prophet who could confess Jesus Christ was God in the flesh was confirming the incarnation and was speaking by the Spirit of God. 1 John 4:2
[2] Hereby know ye the Spirit of God: Every spirit that confesseth that Jesus Christ is come in the flesh is of God.

Now the prophets who would not confess Jesus Christ as God, who denied the incarnation who said Jesus Christ was only a man and not God spoke by the spirit of antichrist. Ironically, we have in the modern Charismatic Movement apostles and prophets who deny the incarnation, teaching Jesus Christ did miracles as a man and not God. They teach against the incarnation saying Jesus Christ laid aside His divinity and walked only as a man in right relationship with God.
The spirit of antichrist working through the first century false prophets was already attacking the deity of Jesus Christ. John was warning Jesus Christ had taught the spirit of antichrist would come and begin to assail the Church. The spirit of antichrist had raised up false

prophets to mislead the Church through false doctrines, and false prophecy.

1 John 4:3
[3] And every spirit that confesseth not that Jesus Christ is come in the flesh is not of God: and this is that spirit of antichrist, whereof ye have heard that it should come; and even now already is it in the world.

Apostle John wanted to expose the false prophets in their midst. John said the indwelling Holy Spirit would lead them to overcome the false prophets. As the spirit of antichrist in the world would be exposed by the greater one inside God's children, the Holy Spirit. In this way the promise of overcoming the false prophets was a certainty as long as God's children were willing to test the spirits of the prophets.

The greater one God the Holy Spirit will defeat the spirit of antichrist and keep God's children from falling into deception by the presence of false prophets in their midst.
1 John 4:4
[4] Ye are of God, little children, and have overcome them: because greater is he that is in you, than he that is in the

The False prophets speak like the world as the spirit of antichrist motivates their doctrines and teachings. As the speak from the spirit of the world, the world will listen and follow in agreement to what they say.

The children of God have been called out from the world and are of God, and so will follow and listen to the doctrines of Jesus Christ and are being led of the Holy Spirit.

1 John 4:5-6
[5] They are of the world: therefore, speak they of the world, and the world heareth them.
[6] We are of God: he that knoweth God heareth us; he that is not of God heareth not us. Hereby know we the spirit of truth, and the spirit of error.

In no way should false prophets be considered a part of the ministry of the Church. The false prophets will not listen to correction and stop seducing the Church. False prophets want to seduce the Church for their own personally gain. False prophets will not listen to apostolic doctrines which have become the infallible Word of God. The false prophets will not submit the written Word of God as their final authority and make their own private interpretations the final authority for their lives. Herby we can know the spirit of truth from the spirit of error. Many false prophets profess they serve the Lord but bring in the antichrist spirit leading the Church into apostasy.

The Apostle Peter Warns of False Prophets
2 Peter 2
The apostle Peter gives one of the strongest detailed
warnings of false prophets and teachers in the New
Testament. Peter reminds the Church in times past the
false prophets mislead the nation of Israel. Peter says
related to the false prophets are the false teachers who
bring in their destructive teachings. Peter uses very
strong language when describing the teachings of false
prophets, and teachers in the New Testament Church.
Peter says their teachings are "damnable heresies" a
twisting of Gods written word which leads those who
follow them into destruction.

1But there were false prophets also among the people,
even as there shall be false teachers among you, who
privily shall bring in damnable heresies, even denying
the Lord that bought them, and bring upon themselves
swift destruction.

These heresies lead the Church into apostasy by denying
the Lord, and the work of the Cross. The end result of
teaching a false Gospel is to bring swift destruction
upon its messengers. Either now in this life, or at the
Judgment Seat of Christ.

2 And many shall follow their pernicious ways; by reason
of whom the way of truth shall be evil spoken of.

Many Christians are drawn apart from the Lord by reason of false prophets, and false doctrines of Church leaders and teachers. Many who profess faith in Christ will follow their destructive ways. In the end all this hypocrisy will end in the mockery of the Lord when their lies and deception are uncovered.

The motivation of false prophets is covetousness, as they are always using fake promises and seductive speech to make a profit off the Church. False prophets want to use the Church to gain the worlds fame and riches. The abuse of the Church brings dire condemnation from the Lord, whose judgment is not afar off, and their damnation is not asleep.

³ And through covetousness shall they with feigned words make merchandise of you: whose judgment now of a long time lingereth not, and their damnation slumbereth not.

Peter then goes on to describe the certainty of Gods judgment against the false prophets comparing God's judgment with the past. Peter reminds the Church how God chained up the angels in Noah's day who left their first estate to take wives from man. God has delivered these angels into the deepest Hell reserving them for the Day of eternal damnation.

Also, Peter reminded the Church about the deluge of waters in the days of Noah where only eight souls were saved alive. Only Noah a preacher of righteousness was saved, while the world mocked his preaching.

Also, how God judged Sodom and Gomorrah condemning them to ashes as they rejected the council of God from Lot. God would only preserve the one righteous man and his family from the fire and brimstone.

4 For if God spared not the angels that sinned, but cast them down to hell, and delivered them into chains of darkness, to be reserved unto judgment;
5 And spared not the old world, but saved Noah the eighth person, a preacher of righteousness,
6 And turning the cities of Sodom and Gomorrha into ashes condemned them with an overthrow, making them an ensample unto those that after should live ungodly;   7 And delivered just Lot, vexed with the filthy conversation of the wicked:
8 (For that righteous man dwelling among them, in seeing and hearing, vexed his righteous soul from day to day with their unlawful deeds;)

Peter then talks about how God preserves the righteous, while delivering the wicked unto the Day of Judgment to be punished. For God knows how to deliver the Godly from the wicked and perverse. In this case false prophets in the Church.

⁹ The Lord knoweth how to deliver the godly out of temptations, and to reserve the unjust unto the day of judgment to be punished:

Peter then goes on to describe the corruption of false prophets and false teachers in the Church. Of the greatest of judgments will come for those who are 1) walking after the lust of uncleanness. 2) Despise government 3) presumptuous and self-willed 4) They refuse to submit to God's authority and end up speaking against any who would expose their rebellion and perversion. Even angels of God who are greater in authority, in power and might do not speak evil against authorities.

¹⁰ But chiefly them that walk after the flesh in the lust of uncleanness and despise government. Presumptuous are they, self-willed, they are not afraid to speak evil of dignities.
¹¹ Whereas angels, which are greater in power and might, bring not railing accusation.

These false prophets are beastly in nature, like wild animals which cannot be tamed. For after their great destructive ways are meant to be taken and destroyed like a dangerous wild beast. God will bring the false prophets to an utter end, as they shall perish in their own corruption.

[12] But these, as natural brute beasts, made to be taken and destroyed, speak evil of the things that they understand not; and shall utterly perish in their own corruption.

Here is strong warning many false prophets are related to the Church by being a brother in Christ. So, what has happened? They will give an account at the Judgment Seat of Christ and receive the reward of the unrighteous. Their hypocrisy will come to light, as they are spots and blemishes in our love feasts.

They are rioting right in the day light, are self-deceived thinking their corruption will have no consequences. Having eyes full of adultery want to beguile unstable souls, having a heart of evil unbelief hardened by covetous practices. Cursed children who have brought the judgment of God upon their apostasy.

[13] And shall receive the reward of unrighteousness, as they that count it pleasure to riot in the daytime. Spots they are and blemishes, sporting themselves with their own deceivings while they feast with you;
[14] Having eyes full of adultery, and that cannot cease from sin; beguiling unstable souls: a heart they have exercised with covetous practices; cursed children:

False prophets who have forsaken the right way and are gone out of the way. Liken unto the false prophet Balaam who loved the riches of the unrighteous. Actions which caused the people of God to stumble. God used the voice of Balaam's donkey to rebuke the madness of the false prophet.

15 Which have forsaken the right way, and are gone astray, following the way of Balaam the son of Bosor, who loved the wages of unrighteousness;
16 But was rebuked for his iniquity: the dumb ass speaking with man's voice forbad the madness of the prophet against them before the Lord.

Concerning gifts and boasting of supernatural abilities, the false prophets are wells without water. Run dry from the Holy Spirit long ago and cannot bring the refreshing waters of the Holy Spirit to the Church. Clouds of a storm which have no rain to bring life into the Church, only destructive winds. The judgment of the outer darkness is reserved against the false prophets.

17 These are wells without water, clouds that are carried with a tempest; to whom the mist of darkness is reserved for ever.

For the prophets speak great swelling words to a man's flesh, his ego, to allure through the lusts of the flesh. Alluring man by his own carnal tendencies. Those in the Church who are clean can escape these powerful corruptors.

18 For when they speak great swelling words of vanity, they allure through the lusts of the flesh, through much

wantonness, those that were clean escaped from them who live in error.

Here in lies the fact many false prophets were once those who followed the Lord. For after they escaped the pollutions of the world by saving faith, the knowledge which comes by the Gospel of Salvation. They are entangled again, and overcome, they have fallen to Satan's snare, and their latter end is worse with them than what they were originally saved from.

They are like dogs who have gone back to their vomit, and pigs who return to their wallowing in the mud. Sadly, it would have been better to have not known the Lord's commandment, than to turn from it after coming to know the Lord. For by their wickedness, they have turned many from the Lord. Their judgment awaits, as many will testify of their corruption before the Lord.

[19] While they promise them liberty, they themselves are the servants of corruption: for of whom a man is overcome, of the same is he brought in bondage.
[20] For if after they have escaped the pollutions of the world through the knowledge of the Lord and Saviour Jesus Christ, they are again entangled therein, and overcome, the latter end is worse with them than the beginning.
[21] For it had been better for them not to have known the way of righteousness, than, after they have known

it, to turn from the holy commandment delivered unto them.

Apostles and Prophets
Understanding the 5-Fold Ministry

Perhaps in this time a great deal of misunderstanding surrounds the doctrine of the 5-Fold ministry. Drawing from Ephesians 4, modern day Charismatics attempt to teach a restoration of the Church through the 5-fold ministry. Especially the belief in a restored apostle, and prophet. Usually, Charismatic Restoration Theology centers around the apostle and prophet being the true form of Church government which replaces the Pastor as a failed one-man form of Church government. Which has led to Charismatic apostolic networks of Churches which are submitted under the authority of the head apostle of their particular Church network. Some apostles have boasted thousands of Churches have come under their authority in apostolic networks. Charismatic leaders say their networks of Churches is the true Church government. By which apostles will spread their apostolic organizations as the Kingdom of heaven all over the world before Jesus Christ can return.

First of all, the foundation of the Church is not founded upon modern day apostles and prophets. The foundation had already been laid in the apostle Paul's day, by the original 12 apostles of the Lamb, and the apostle Paul who wrote the infallible Word of God. Included are the prophets of Old as recorded in the Scriptural passages of the Old Testament whose prophetic words are also the infallible written Word of God. So modern day apostles and prophets are inferior in that they can only build upon the foundation which has already been laid by the original apostles and prophets. With Jesus Christ being the Corner Stone of the foundation.

One of the major deceptions is to make modern day apostles and prophets the foundational government of the Church. As the Churches foundation was already established almost two thousand years ago, modern day apostles and prophets can only build upon the foundation which has already been laid. The apostle Paul showed the pattern of laying the foundation in birthing new Churches, a foundation which was the Gospel of Jesus Christ. After a local Church had been founded, Paul would appoint local Church elders who were to govern the Church. Paul never attempted to govern new Churches by an apostolic network or building a denomination under his name or authority. Paul recognized the Church was to be governed at a local level, with each Church having its own local government led by Church elders. As apostle Paul did the work of an apostle, it required his constant travel so Paul could not govern the Church by reason of his absence.

Apostles and prophets are not Church government, as long as they are required to move about from place to place. Instead, elders appointed by the Holy Spirit on a local basis are the true government of the local Church. Imagine modern apostles who have collected thousands of Churches into their apostolic networks where they may never even step one foot into anyone of those Churches. They are Church collectors and marketers of Churches in which they never birthed and claim authority over other men's labors.

Many boast of their apostleship but were not sent by God to collect Churches and establish new Church networks. Most move from conference to conference as speakers, and in Christian environments with those who are already saved and pray for the sick and boast miracles are the sign of their apostleship. So much pretense has come out of self-declared apostles as they imagine God has given them the authority to make the Kingdom of heaven on earth before Jesus Christ can return. Their philosophy is apostolic/prophetic government is the new wineskin by which the Holy Spirit can pour the fullness of His power. Not as in other ages when Pastors and local Church elders governed the Church, considered old worn-out wineskins which could never hold the full power of the Holy Spirit to govern the world making the nations Christian before Christ can return.

All this exaltation and elitism has led to an enormous amount of false prophecy, and the largest decline of Christianity in America during their supposed takeover of the world. Real apostles and prophets have always existed since the formation of the New Testament Church, as well as false apostles and false prophets. Exalting the apostolic and prophetic in these days has led to thousands of men and women to say they are an apostle or prophet, but do not fulfill the Biblical character of those ministries. These pretenders have proven to be a great source of deception inside the Charismatic Movement.

Ephesians 4:7-16
[7] But unto every one of us is given grace according to the measure of the gift of Christ.   [8] Wherefore he saith, When he ascended up on high, he led captivity captive, and gave gifts unto men.
[9] (Now that he ascended, what is it but that he also descended first into the lower parts of the earth?
[10] He that descended is the same also that ascended up far above all heavens, that he might fill all things.)
[11] And he gave some, apostles; and some, prophets; and some, evangelists; and some, pastors and teachers;
[12] For the perfecting of the saints, for the work of the ministry, for the edifying of the body of Christ:
[13] Till we all come in the unity of the faith, and of the knowledge of the Son of God, unto a perfect man, unto the measure of the stature of the fulness of Christ:

¹⁴ That we henceforth be no more children, tossed to and fro, and carried about with every wind of doctrine, by the sleight of men, and cunning craftiness, whereby they lie in wait to deceive;

¹⁵ But speaking the truth in love, may grow up into him in all things, which is the head, even Christ:

¹⁶ From whom the whole body fitly joined together and compacted by that which every joint supplieth, according to the effectual working in the measure of every part, maketh increase of the body unto the edifying of itself in love.

Restoration of Apostles and Prophets

Back twenty years ago the Charismatic Movement was beginning to emphasize the ministry of the apostle. One self-declared apostle pushed the philosophy of apostles and prophets are the true government of the Church. This self-declared apostle believed the Book of Revelation was already 90 % fulfilled in history, so only a golden age of the Church remained. With his Preterist eschatology in hand went about to teach how God was restoring marketplace apostles and prophets to transform culture making it Christian before Jesus Christ would return. Today, his philosophy has advanced as marketplace apostles have morphed into the 7 Mountain Mandate, a philosophy promoted by a disciple of the apostle. His disciple has adopted restored marketplace apostles and prophets into the 7 Mountain

Gospel. Both men believed restored apostles and prophets are the Church government as in comparison to Pastors and local Church elders. 7 Mountain apostles and prophets have formed associations of Churches which would submit to an apostle, or team of apostles to have proper Church government and authority. Eventually the apostle coined a term for these Church networks calling the Movement the New Apostolic Reformation. (NAR)

Today many Charismatic who hold the values of restored apostles and prophets attempt to distance themselves from any recognition of the New Apostolic Reformation. The original issue was all the "new doctrines" which came with the New Apostolic Reformation (NAR). For example, Dominion Theology, where the NAR teaches God has restored the lost dominion Adam had in the Garden. This resorted dominion was then to fit into the "new apostolic wineskins," which replaced the worn out one-man pastoral wineskins which could never contain the fulness of the Holy Spirit. Of course, the superior government of apostles and prophets would carry greater power and authority to transform culture making for Christian cities and nations. Too much his demise the apostle who formed the NAR admitted after 20 years of the New Apostolic Reformation, no city or nation had actually been transformed by apostolic prophetic government.

What is the problem? The whole notion of restored apostles and prophets for a superior Church government and worldwide cultural transformation is based upon philosophy and not fact. The New Apostolic Reformation was formed by manmade efforts on false doctrinal beliefs.

Charismatic Restoration philosophy is made up, and not according to what has already been written. God choose apostles and prophets almost two thousand years before the formation of the NAR. Throughout Church history there has always been God ordained apostles and prophets in the New Testament Church. Even though not recognized by the organized Catholic Church, apostles and prophets still functioned in their calling and ministries throughout Church history. Well, it is true the Catholic Church has perverted Church government, it is equally true God in not restoring Church government by apostolic networks. Gods Church has always been government on a local Church level by God ordained elders. In this case the New Apostolic Reformation is just another man-made perversion of Church government. The Catholic Church has its Pope, while the NAR has its apostolic popes.

What is Restoration Theology based upon? The real Scriptural teaching on restoration has nothing to do with the restoration of modern-day marketplace apostles and prophets. The true teaching given by the original apostles like Peter, was in the last days God would restore the nation of Israel once again, as the head of all nations. This is the true teaching on restored government, as Jesus Christ will return and set up His Millennial Kingdom on earth with Israel as the place of His Throne. The work of restoration being done by God is called the "Fallen Tabernacle of David," where God will draw all nations once again by Christ setting up His government upon earth during the Millennium, in the New Jerusalem.

As you can see the government which transforms the world comes at the Second Coming of Jesus Christ and the restoration of Israel. Restoration Theology as taught by the NAR is a complete corruption of the Written Word of God. It has nothing to do with Church government and apostolic networks. Makes you wonder why so many modern-day apostles attempt to deny their connection to the New Apostolic Reformation. So, inside the Movement even attempt has come to deny the NAR is just a "conspiracy theory," created by those who have exposed the false doctrines and practices of apostles and prophets of the NAR.

Acts 15:12-17

[12] Then all the multitude kept silence, and gave audience to Barnabas and Paul, declaring what miracles and wonders God had wrought among the Gentiles by them. [13] And after they had held their peace, James answered,

saying, Men and brethren, hearken unto me:
[14] Simeon hath declared how God at the first did visit
the Gentiles, to take out of them a people for his name.
[15] And to this agree the words of the prophets; as it is
written,   [16] After this I
will return, and will build again the tabernacle of David,
which is fallen down; and I will build again the ruins
thereof, and I will set it up:
[17] That the residue of men might seek after the Lord,
and all the Gentiles, upon whom my name is called,
saith the Lord, who doeth all these things.

Amos 9:8-13

Behold, the eyes of the Lord GOD are upon the sinful
kingdom, and I will destroy it from off the face of the
earth; saving that I will not utterly destroy the house of
Jacob, saith the LORD.
[9] For, lo, I will command, and I will sift the house of
Israel among all nations, like as corn is sifted in a sieve,
yet shall not the least grain fall upon the earth.
[10] All the sinners of my people shall die by the sword,
which say, The evil shall not overtake nor prevent us.
[11] In that day will I raise up the tabernacle of David that
is fallen and close up the breaches thereof; and I will
raise up his ruins, and I will build it as in the days of old:
[12] That they may possess the remnant of Edom, and of
all the heathen, which are called by my name, saith
the LORD that doeth this.
[13] Behold, the days come, saith the LORD, that the

plowman shall overtake the reaper, and the treader of grapes him that soweth seed; and the mountains shall drop sweet wine, and all the hills shall melt.

Apostles and Prophets At Judgment Seat
Church history demonstrates the corruption of the Church by false doctrines and corrupted leaders. Self-proclaimed apostles and prophets have from the very beginning been a great source of deception. All the original apostles warned the Church of false apostles and prophets. So even in the first century the Church was already being invaded by corrupted doctrines and leaders. The apostle Paul warn specifically in the last days a Great Apostasy would come by the influences of doctrines of demons and the seduction of corrupted leaders. As the last days represents a great peril of corrupted leaders the Church should hold fast to testing the spirit of its leaders. However, many leaders have taught against the Scriptures and have created a following based upon their own revelations and private interpretations. In this way the Church has been divided into sects, were men follow the false doctrines and practices of exalted apostles and prophets. Today the Charismatic Church has been divided up along these sects with an exalted apostle at the head of the organization.

Now what will be the outcome of apostles and prophets who are leading the Church into deception? All who proclaim faith in Christ must stand before God In judgement. At the Second Coming of Jesus Christ all who are born again must meet with the Lord at the "Bema Seat," where God will measure one's life works after coming In saving faith. So, no man can stand before God and declare his own works were for the glory of God. Instead, the judicial fires of Christ will test the quality of everyman's works to see what manner they really are. Only the fire of God can reveal the true quality of the saints works. Of gold, silver, precious stones, or wood, hay, and stubble.

Conclusion
Is the Prophetic Word Lost In Charismatics?

Having been part of the prophetic ministry since the early 1980's I want to send out a challenge to the Charismatics. My challenge comes from my experience inside the Movement where I see the prophetic word of God has been shut out from the Movement. I do not mean there are not thousands of Charismatics who proclaim they are prophetic, or thousands of prophecies given every year. Instead, of the absence of prophetic ministry there is a super abundance. Here in lies the problem and the proof the Prophetic Word of the Lord has been shut out. The magnitude of false prophecies, and false predictive words outweighs and numbers any true prophetic word a thousand to one. When a false word is given and marketed as a prophetic word from God, and the Charismatics accept the false, then a spirit of error has seduced Christians into accepting deception. The Scriptures are clear a prophetic word comes from the inspiration of the Holy Spirit and is the testimony of Jesus which is the Spirit of prophecy. A false prophetic word does not come from the Holy Spirit, does not have its origin from God, and can deceive Christians into following a lie. The end result of false prophetic words are self-willed Christians walking by works of the flesh, or demonic spirits but are considered the Spirit of Truth.

In these days, a pure prophetic word from God in the Charismatic Movement is rare. What stands in the way, are beliefs which are not confronted by the Movement. Here are a few:

1) Prophetic Words which speak of judgement or warning are considered words of doom and old fashioned. Words which are confrontative and corrective in nature are shut out by in large as they are considered negative and focus on sin instead of victory. A philosophical belief in a Triumphant Church without deep sin, and demonic deception is being promoted. Despite the facts of great sin in the body of Christ, and falling leaders, an agreement of non-confrontation is set in place. The emergence of a "no judgment theology" has put a positive mental attitude in place of corrective prophetic words or prophetic words which warn or correct. As the Bible describes basic preaching as

confrontational, corrective, and even rebuke, the Spirit of God is not allowed to move in this very basic way.

2 Timothy 4:1-4
1 I charge thee therefore before God, and the Lord Jesus Christ, who shall judge the quick and the dead at his appearing and his kingdom;
2 Preach the word; be instant in season, out of season; reprove, rebuke, exhort with all longsuffering and doctrine.
3 For the time will come when they will not endure sound doctrine; but after their own lusts shall they heap to themselves teachers, having itching ears;
4 And they shall turn away their ears from the truth and shall be turned unto fables.

2) What stands out about the Spirit of God in the prophets is the corrective nature of prophetic words. Have you seen one of the primary aspects of prophets is to confront error and deception? To bring warning about living right with God. The prophets have been given the responsibility as "watchmen," and are to set the Trumpet of God to their mouths to blow the Trumpet in warning God's people. The Spirit of Truth exposes the Spirit of error amidst God's people, calling them out of deception into repentance and back to God. That is why there

are so few true prophetic words allowed in the modern Charismatic Movement today. As the numbers of leaders who proclaim the have the anointing from God, lack the ability to bring correction and exposure to the Spirit of Error running rampant throughout the Charismatic Movement.

3) Even Charisma Magazine in one article out of one hundred will even admit to the sin and deception going on inside the Movement. However, the popular theology of the day is a no judgement, a Super Church without any defeat.So, these articles are mainly swept under the carpet by the magnitude of optimistic philosophies.

4) Another factor which has suppressed the true prophetic Word of the Lord is called the Extreme Prophetic. It consists of the marketing of "so called heavenly encounters." Which are just marketed a visions or visitations from angels, or dead people in heaven, or visiting heaven itself. In this style of prophetic "it's not about Gods Word," instead it is about the supernatural experience itself. The fact you were taken into heaven or spoke to an angel or dead saint. In fact, the information given about these encounters is usually extreme and outlandish. Supernatural experiences which almost never

bring real exposure, or correction. Instead, the Spirit of Error has multiplied lying visions and visitations by the thousands.

No prophetic word is given, just as spiritual badge to say, "I am favored by God, and you should come to my meetings so you can have these experiences too."

What is the end result? All the multiplied thousands of false prophetic ministry has replaced the prophetic watchmen, and the word of the Lord. If you are prophetic just ask yourself why God almost never shows you anything wrong with the Church today? Also why are Charismatic leaders who hold popular platforms today hold to a philosophy of no correction, no confrontation, no rebuke, and no future judgement, or exposure of sin?

Isaiah 58:1-2
1 Cry aloud, spare not, lift up thy voice like a trumpet, and shew my people their transgression, and the house of Jacob their sins. 2 Yet they seek me daily, and delight to know my ways, as a nation that did righteousness, and forsook not the ordinance of their God: they ask of me the ordinances of justice; they take delight in approaching to God.

What Has Happened Since False Trump Prophecies?

2020 exposed what has been a chronic problem inside the Charismatic Movement, mainly false prophetic words. For years Christians outside the Charismatic Movement have confronted self-declared prophets with giving volumes of false prophecies. Most of these confrontations were basically ignored by the prophetic, justifying to themselves those Christians simply do not believe in the gifts of the Holy Spirit like prophecy, or tongues. However, many times the case was simply prophetic words violated the written Word of God, or simply were false predictions which did not happen. In 2020 the Charismatic Prophetic was exposed by all the failed predictions of the President Trump reelection.

For a while, all the false predictions drew a lot of attention even from major news sources which exposed the false and lying predictive prophetic words. Inside the Charismatic Movement many Christians simply refused to let go and were reproving anyone who was admitting they gave false prophecy. In many cases a great divide manifested between Charismatics who were angry at one another for any admittance of compromise. For those self-styled prophets who confessed their prophetic words were false, other Charismatics would rebuke them in anger for giving up on their Trump prophetic reelection predictions. One well know prophet who confessed false prophetic predictions was threatened with death and harm to his family.

What has happened since all these calamities have had some time to pass? If any Christian or individuals outside the Church is looking for major confrontation, or reform you will be sorely disappointed. If you are look for a major high-profile leader rebuking the deception and calling for major oversight you will not find it. If you look for a well know Charismatic theologian exposing the falsehood, the list will be short, namely RT. Kindell who rebuked the Prophetic say God was angry at all the false prophecy. What was ironic, many leaders who have been called false prophets by those outside the Movement, attempted to teach against false prophecy and false prophets. They were the chief offenders yet would not apply those teachings to themselves. Dr Michael Brown said before the results of the election, if these prophets were proven false then there is a problem of major deception inside the Movement.

How serious is the issue? Enough to be mocked and ridiculed by the world as right-wing extremists who had a cult like devotion to President Trump. Inside the Church the prevailing presence of false prophecy, should sound the alarm of false prophets in their midst. However, this is not the belief or alarm by those inside the Prophetic Movement. Here is what being modeled:

1) No major prophetic voice has called for reform in prophecy, or among those who claim to be prophets.
2) For those who have a reputation of being a prophet inside the Movement, false prophecy is just part of what they do.
3) Testing of spirits to see if false prophets are in their midst is not part of the Movement.
4) Testing of prophecy is an afterthought. When false prophecy is given, it is never brought out and confronted. Instead, it has been buried in the past.
5) When a prophetic word is given, it is more about the sensation it creates among Charismatics, as compared as to its actually being true.
6) In reality false prophecy has proven to be manmade, or even philosophical beliefs which are spoken in the name of the Lord.

All these practices have been normalized inside the Prophetic Movement and have not changed with the 2020 false prophecy exposure. I trust as no Charismatic leader is calling for reform, all these things will continue as if no issue has ever existed.

1 Corinthians 14:31-40

[31] For ye may all prophesy one by one, that all may learn, and all may be comforted.   [32] And the spirits of the prophets are subject to the prophets.
[33] For God is not the author of confusion, but of peace,

as in all churches of the saints.   ³⁴ Let your women keep silence in the churches: for it is not permitted unto them to speak; but they are commanded to be under obedience as also saith the law.   ³⁵ And if they will learn anything, let them ask their husbands at home: for it is a shame for women to speak in the church.

³⁶ What? came the word of God out from you? or came it unto you only?   ³⁷ If any man think himself to be a prophet, or spiritual, let him acknowledge that the things that I write unto you are the commandments of the Lord.

³⁸ But if any man be ignorant, let him be ignorant.

³⁹ Wherefore, brethren, covet to prophesy, and forbid not to speak with tongues.

⁴⁰ Let all things be done decently and in order.

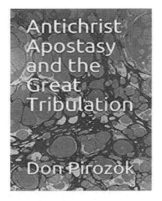

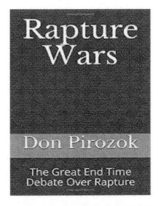

Made in the USA
Middletown, DE
27 December 2021

57123524R00144